Animals Strike Curious Poses

Animals Strike Curious Poses
Essays
Elena Passarello

Sarabande Books
Louisville, KY | Brooklyn, NY

439 7176

Library of Congress Cataloging-in-Publication Data

Names: Passarello, Elena, author.
Title: Animals strike curious poses : essays / by Elena Passarello.
Description: First edition. | Louisville, KY : Sarabande Books, [2017]
Identifiers: LCCN 2016039498 | ISBN 9781941411391 (hardcover)
Classification: LCC PS3616.A856 A6 2017 | DDC 814/.6--dc23
LC record available at https://lccn.loc.gov/2016039498

Interior and exterior design by Kristen Radtke.

Manufacured in Canada.
This book is printed on acid-free paper.

Sarabande Books is a nonprofit literary organization.

This project is supported in part by an award from the National Endowment for the Arts. The Kentucky Arts Council, the state arts agency, supports Sarabande Books with state tax dollars and federal funding from the National Endowment for the Arts.

For Pizza Rat.

Just kidding. For David.

Contents

Year by year,
the monkey's mask
reveals the monkey.
          —Bashō

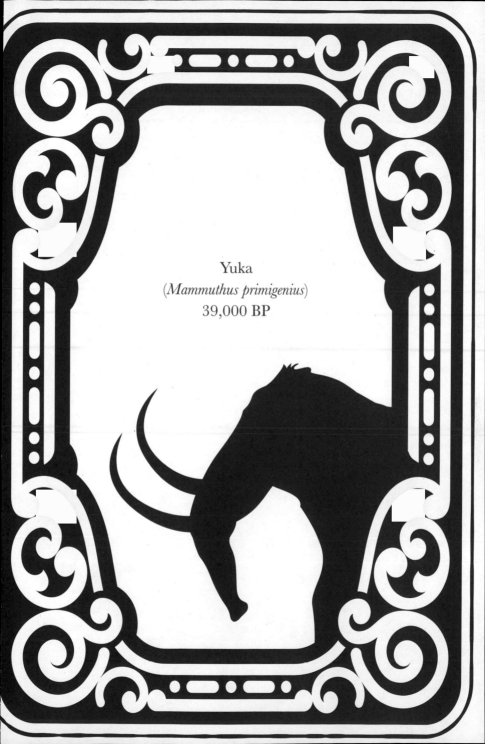

Yuka
(*Mammuthus primigenius*)
39,000 BP

Even more interesting, there are hints that humans may have taken over
the kill at an early stage.
Professor Daniel Fisher, 2012

They have been here!
Eliette Brunel in Chauvet Cave, 1994

HE FOUND THE MAMMOTH IN the rock-hard earth.

She lay at the top of the continent, near a sea that thaws in July and refreezes by September. It was a tusk hunter who spotted her, upside-down, in the half-frozen crag. First a rock, then a rock in the shape of a foot and a flank and a hollowed-out eye. Her trunk extended down the crag like a pull-chain.

Quickly, he could see that, as if by some ancient magic, she was still woolly. Red-blonde fetlocks clung to her feet, her haunches, to the rock that kept her. It was thick and vibrant, the kind you'd see on a ginger-haired dime-store doll. The hunter who chiseled her from the permafrost—we think he was named Vasily—kept quiet about his process, but no matter the work, it was too easy a task. Cutting away thirty-nine thousand years should cost a monument of labor. Instead, as payment, he pushed a silver earring into the thawing silt.

The rock that had kept her for millennia was four days' journey from anything road-like, so Vasily assembled a posse, tied her to a snowmobile, and got down to it. The summer thaw did little to speed their sledge from Yukagir toward the mountains, and somewhere between the Laptev Sea and the village of Ust-Kuyga, she thawed a bit, loosening to the temperature of the living for about three days. They finally parked the slab he'd dragged her on, still nine hundred miles north of the coldest city on the planet, in an undisclosed ice cave: sped from one frozen home to another to await the highest bidder.

Vasily and company figured that any twenty-first-century human—science-mole, ivory-hawk, or adventure-hound—once he crawled into the cave and pulled back the blue tarps that swaddled her? He'd bite at the first sight of that Pleistocene wool. Because uncovering a mammoth in a frozen cave does something to a neocortex. Since language is epically younger than both thought and experience, "woolly mammoth" means, to a human brain, something more like time. It might mean time even more than "time" does, since a brain's chance of holding any span of years is laughable. Few bodies have felt the real pull of a century and fewer brains can grasp ten, even in dreams. What, asks the brain, is tangible in one hundred years, let alone a century repeated four hundred times?

And so a frozen mammoth means more than one gray, unspined back on a slab in a cave, rounded feet pointing at the ice-roof. More than sliding a gloved palm under that fiery wool and more than patting that trunk where it curves, as if in trumpet. More than running a glove along that corkscrewed flank to find a large and peculiar gash, made by—what did *that*? Not teeth or claw, but some sort of serrated tool—the kind held in a fleshy palm and steadied by an opposable thumb.

•• ▬ • ▬ ••

Of all the images that make our world, animal images are particularly buried inside us. We feel the pull of them before we know to name them, or how to even fully see them. It is as if they are always waiting, crude sketches of themselves, in the recesses of our bodies. As if every animal a human brain has ever seen, it has swallowed. We find their outlines, as if on Ouija boards, in mountains and in clouds. We scratch the arcs of their trunks in the dirt with our feet, or use the sharpest tools available to dig them from shocks of wood. Give us a stick and we'll draw them. Find a discarded antler on the steppe and we'll locate them in its tines. Hit a rock on a cave wall until it yields one. Spread them out across the night sky and we'll point upward. See how they twinkle as they move?

Up from the mummy on that ice-cave slab comes a linked chain of animals, all of them pointing backward. That spineless knot of feet and fur untwists into an upright beast with movable legs and an intact, champing maw. She reinflates inside the humans that touch her as a circus pachyderm or an elephantine nursery toy. Further inward still, she is the image of a cutout suspended over a bassinet for eyes too new to focus, the curves and lines of her paper feet trotting at the ends of the wires. And perhaps the red-haired mammoth, which someone in the cave named Yuka, takes the onlookers further back still, to memories buried not in the brain, but in marrow and fiber and peptide. Far into the flesh, where the temporal world starts to wobble a bit.

Thirty-nine thousand years ago, young Yuka set off running. She could have run for her natural life—the land, as it was then, gave her the space to do so. She might have traveled the entire length of the steppe, had she wanted to. If she'd headed east out of what wasn't yet Yukagir, she could run to what wasn't yet Fairbanks. There was no ocean to stop her and barely any trees, just the hardscrabble forbs she yanked from the permafrost with that custom-made fist in her trunk. Or she could have run south for twice that distance—alone or in packs, always traveling, feet visible in the speed-reel of passing millennia as fuzzy blurs of motion. Eight thousand miles of dodging deadly silt bogs and the canny lions that followed her, growing hungrier as they, too, ran down eight thousand miles of cold. Not the same lions as now, exactly, but still leonine and speedy-moving things. Still the same sun, though brighter in the frigid sky. Still a continent, but one triple the size, its land sitting on half the planet like a fat cave bear.

And all around the lip of the steppe ran an impossible mix of fauna. A near-bestiary moving over what was not yet Europe: reindeer and hyena, bear and lion, jungle leopard and arctic fox. All the imaginable animals running alongside her, following those rivers that cut soft, deep caves through miles of limestone. Past things we now call meadows and things that were not yet ponds and things that, in essence, were men.

A silent hunter crouches in an up-jump of the steppe. More than any physical act—fighting, teaching, sleep—his life is spent watching animals. Survival is hiding his soft human body and clocking the heartier megafauna as they move and mate and perish. Imagine the detail he holds inside himself after a lifetime of fiery looking. Then think of five thousand such lifetimes, all spent on that steppe and at this pitch of watching. Good God, what that amount of witness must do to a human's insides.

To be human on the steppe was to hold a codex of every muscle in a lion's neck, a bison's spine, a caballine flank running to safety. Before it became anything else, a human brain was first an almanac of living shapes changing in the passing light: living shapes in the chaos of estrus, the lurch of paucity, the freeze of death. How could a creature hold such continental knowledge— generations of it—and not feel it seeping into his blood and bones and muscles? How many generations of hunters pass by before such watching troubles a hunter's body into hysteria, or drunkenness—the animal shapes thrumming so hard at his ribcage that he must seek release outside himself?

When the red-blonde mammoth runs into eyeshot, the hunter tenses. Her wool in the rising sun seems as if it might catch fire. She's grown enough to have her own space in the herd, but still young enough to be toppled, and as she moves, it is easy to see that her rhythm is off. That rhythm tells the hunter of the predators that got to her first. She turns to charge the lion that chases her, but only manages one belabored stamp of her thick, round foot before panicking. The mammoth turns to keep running, and her foot snaps; soon the leg will give.

Go now, thinks the hunter, imagining himself into the lion's body, and the lion seems to listen to him. It springs sideways onto the mammoth's back—the first bite, at her tail, is enough. The deep scratches it leaves along her sides will have no time to heal. She wrenches her fiery blonde neck, twisting herself away from the bite, and falls with a little thud.

And now it is time for the human hunter to make good on all his watching. To move forward—not running, but with firm and even paces: arm up, weapon out. He must bluff the lion into retreating. It's a move the hunter has stolen from the lion itself after years together on the steppe. To steal from the lion, he becomes the lion. *Go now*, he says again—to his own body this time. He finds the rhythm of the lion inside him and brings it forward.

The lion runs away, its four feet a tawny blur. The hunter knows how little time it takes for a lion to remember its power, so the work here is quick: a hand on the mammoth's still-hot flank and a sharp edge dug into her spine. He pulls only the most useful parts from her: vertebrae, organs, the fat and meat from her legs. For some reason, he extracts the skull, but does not take it with him. He buries it, and what else is left, into the steppe to return to later. At this point in time, he has no idea how much later that will be.

That gash on Yuka's back is thirty-four thousand years older than the first version of Stonehenge. It's thirty-three thousand years before anything resembling writing, and at least thirty millennia before beer, knitting, money, or apiaries. Yuka's sharp wound is nearly as old as the bone flutes recently dug from German rock—the ones that can whistle the pentatonic sounds of birds in the changing sky—and the lion-headed man that someone carved from a mammoth tusk and abandoned in a cave for forty millennia. Fifteen thousand years after Yuka, mammoth bones will make the first huts and fences and graveyards. The architecture of Europe will be born from the bodies of the mammoths that the first hunters spent eternities watching.

Thirteen millennia after Yuka, a woman—the first known shaman—will lie in a grave with a fox in her arms. Above her body, they'll cross two mammoth scapulae and dust the bones with yellow-red ochre. Around her, they'll bury a collection of clay—the first known ceramics—fired into dog shapes, bear shapes, horse shapes, and also the shapes of mammoths.

Around the same time—if there is even any reason to call this "time"—a hunter will walk to a river cave, alone. Though he's watched animals all his life, he won't hunt them today. Instead, he will search for a giant limestone arch—sturdy and thick on one end, the other end a rounded crag with a narrower offshoot. The arch looks like a mammoth leaping over the river, from rock to rock.

Go now. Go and collect them. Collect them all in a cave hidden by a river, under a leaping mammoth of limestone, where the floor goes five hundred years between sets of footprints. Collect the lion, the rhinoceros, the ibex, the aurochs. The cave bear and the lion and the wolf. Collect them in charcoal and ochre on the sharpened ends of pine boughs. But put the largest animals—the ones held inside the hunters with the deepest-reaching memories—way in the back of the cave. Keep them far from the sunlit art of the carvers and engravers who mold stone and wood into utile things. Find them in the way-back darkness where giant bears go to die.

● ● ▬ ● ▬ ● ●

He walks inside the cave and lights a bough to see what he can gather. There is no space between himself and the ten millennia of his imagination. No distance between the beasts of the outside world and the beasts inside him. The back chamber is tight enough that its air is poisoned by the sighs of tree roots above him. The animals are in his short breath, in the wet tips of his fingers. As the lamplight ripples past the rock, there are lions in the fire.

He puts a hand to that soft wall and there she is, running for eight thousand years. And he becomes the mammoth so he can envision the mammoth, running toward his hand so fast her feet are rounded blurs at the ends of her triangle legs. His palm on the rock and her red fur, the thrum of his heart and the roll of her feet. Their feet. The black of the fire and the black of the bough and the red ochre that frames them both like fur. Their trunk pulling downward and the charcoal gash running the middle of their back. Their brown hand palpitating it all in the limestone, then pulling away.

He has found the mammoth in the rock.

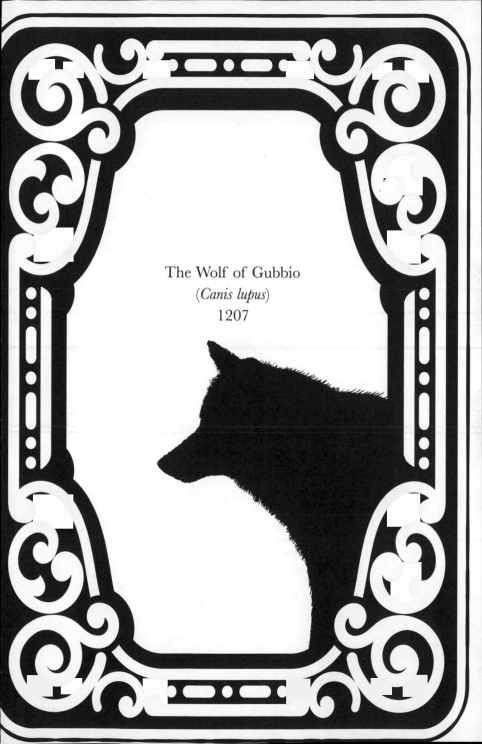

The Wolf of Gubbio
(*Canis lupus*)
1207

Therefore to a man that is suddenly still, and leaveth to speak, it is said,
Lupus est in fabula: "The wolf is in the tale."
Bartholomaeus Anglicus, *On the Nature of Things*

WINTERS WERE EVIL IN GUBBIO. The town was shoved into the lowest spur of a mountain, faced by warring neighbors and terrible winds. The citizens peered from their guard towers into the darkness, beyond the high walls and past the amphitheater that had been moldering near them for a thousand years. They were starving, but did not hunt in their pine forests on account of the Wolf.

This was also the name given to their famine and their plague: *lupus*, the hungry devil always within walking distance of their city gates. For hunger, like the Wolf, takes from you what it needs, and does so with remorselessness and skill. But there were some occasions that evil winter when the people of Gubbio had no choice but to leave the town. Their dead were always buried outside those gates, since the time of the amphitheater, Wolf or no.

A posse comitatus of men and dogs dragged the latest bodies past the empty fields—the sheep and shepherds gone now—and into the frigid woods where they knew the Wolf would find them.

They knew of his night vision and his cocky howl. They knew how well he chased less nimble beasts in the deep snow. They knew that, on bright afternoons, he'd make sport with shepherd boys and then return at twilight to pull them back to his cave. The books said twilight was the time of the Wolf, as the beast devoured the setting sun.

Learned men had kept track of the nature of things since the time of their amphitheater. Their books told of how, in lean seasons, the Wolf ate wind and how he sometimes gobbled mud so he could topple a stag with his weight. They wrote that he cooked the flesh he killed with his hot, acidic breath. If, they said, when stalking, he stepped on a twig and alerted the innocent lamb, he bit his guilty foot as punishment. Here he is, a whole page in the *Bestiarium vocabulum*, sulking in vivid color. Note how the Wolf holds his right paw between his own pointed teeth.

Mostly, the books of beasts used the Wolf to illustrate the most lupine of human sins. You must hate the sins of the Wolf, the bestiaries said—the sins of rogues, apostates, and highwaymen—as they are sins too cunning to simply be feared. Hear these words on the Wolf, sinners, and then think upon the Wolf that might, at any moment, ravage the Lamb inside you.

Up in the woods, the Wolf watched them in the half-light while standing on a frozen grave. He sniffed the air and turned toward the approaching men, even though the bestiaries said wolves could not turn their heads at all—just as the Devil is unable to turn toward righteousness. But the Wolf that came to Gubbio *did* swivel its head to see them, which gave the men horrific pause.

It is written that, when man and Wolf meet, should the Wolf see the man first, the man will fall mute. On one colorful page of the bestiary, the Wolf is ochre and looks no more than a dog. It sneaks up behind a man in a russet tunic; the man holds his hand at his own white chin. If the dumbstruck man survives this encounter—perhaps he will be the only one of his group to do so—the books say his voice may return, but only after he strips naked and claps together two loud stones.

Francesco di Pietro di Bernardone was nearly naked when he arrived in Gubbio. He'd left Assisi in a cast-off cloak, but highwaymen robbed him of it before he reached Valfábbrica. That town was troubled by flood and did not welcome him. In Gubbio, however, he had old friends from the war. They led him in, found him a tunic, told them they'd had no flood. *But we do have a wolf,* they said, and Francis fell silent with prayer.

The men Francis knew in Gubbio noticed great changes in him. They could not decipher it; where before, he was dandy and hot-blooded, now he curled up in the corner, gaunt and still. He swallowed ash before meals to keep himself from savoring food. When his flesh buzzed with pleasure, he jumped into thorny bushes, or retreated to fast in a cave. Comfort was slipping from him like color from a sick girl's face. Francis had willingly let the hunger crawl into his life.

Gubbio's gates opened for him again and he walked out. His soldier-fellows and their dogs followed behind with axes, heading past the amphitheater and up into the woods, where the brush was thick. Soon, though, fear froze them and they were unable to advance. Only Francis, in his thin tunic and rotten shoes, walked on.

It is also written in the bestiary that, if the man sees the Wolf first, the Wolf will lose his rage.

He called out to the Wolf—*Brother!*—before it could turn to face him. He spoke in his odd mix of Latin and Umbrian and perhaps, too, in his special, blessed tongue of wildness. Many stories would soon follow Francis that spoke of this wildness, and how it brought him nearer to his God. Learned men and women would write of how, when he walked the Strada Francesca, he scratched in the dirt to move worms from his path, thus saving them from trampling. Frogs quieted at his sermons, for he knew their language. When he sat in the mud and preached to birds, which was often, he chastised them gently.

Look at you, birds, he said. *You are swaddled in three layers of garment even though you cannot sew a stitch. You neither farm nor hunt, but are always fed. It is a wonder that so little plagues you. Sisters, your only sin could be ingratitude, for so many creatures contend with so much more sin—sin that's bred from a deadlier wanting.*

To the Wolf, however, Francis did not speak of God's generosity. Instead, he said, *Brother! I know your hunger.*

To this, the Wolf answered, *Lo!*

On the front door of the basilica in Assisi is carved a scene of Francis in the woods, opening his hand to the Wolf, which crouches below him. A fresco in the monastery at Saorge has the Wolf skinny like a cat, with three lizard toes—Francis's fingers are raised to the beast in benediction. Four thousand miles away, over the door of the Chapel of Francis and the Wolf, is a lunette bas-relief of him pressing his palm to the beast's forehead. In the garden of Gubbio's Santa Maria della Vittoria stands a stone plaque of the Wolf on its hind legs, forepaws at Francis's shoulders in a kind of embrace. A frontispiece to the *Fioretti di San Francesco* shows the pair approaching the walls of Gubbio, the Wolf heeling at the man's side. And an altarpiece in Sansepolcro depicts the fearful town blocking their gates and a haloed Francis entreating them to clear the way into Gubbio. He holds the Wolf's paw in his hand.

By the end of the winter, Francis had returned to Assisi to beg on the streets for stones. News of his legend traveled back to Gubbio for the next twenty years. That he had found a pack of eleven men to follow him through Umbria; they howled in the woods as they walked from town to town. That, in their ravenous wandering, Francis threw prayers into the wind and gobbled them up for sustenance. That the five wounds of Christ appeared on his body while he starved on a mountainside, hidden in a dark wood rife with thieves. That, two winters after his death, he was already sainted.

By then, Francis in Gubbio was barely a dream, like a story in a book that keeps rewriting itself. The Wolf, however, remained. For two winters after Francis left them, it visited Gubbio weekly. Any time the Wolf approached the gates, they welcomed it with affection. See the canvas in many-colored oils of the Wolf on a Gubbio doorstep, fetching scraps from a merchant. A mother and child look on, a dog sleeps near the Wolf's feet, and Francis's halo floats above the Wolf's head.

But they could not help but notice how greatly the Wolf had changed. A few in the town asked if the creature that came begging at their gates was still indeed a wolf. Does it still eat the wind when it is starving? Does it still hate the sound of clapping stones? Should travelers still sew a wolf's eye on their sleeves to ward off the highwaymen, and should babies still suck on wolf teeth to soothe their gums? They could not decipher it.

They began to wonder if hunger was the only difference between a devil and a dog. And since the Wolf was now something else, they wondered about the man who'd convinced them to tame it. If the Wolf is no wolf and Francis no longer a man, what did that make Gubbio?

Their books told them nothing. It was not in their nature to answer this kind of inquiry. Those pages merely arranged the animal world—illustrated it—as a strange and unwieldy place filled with hunger and cunning, goodness and lechery. Choose one creature to honor, the books said, and one to hope you'll never let inside yourself. Be the pilgrim, not the highwayman. Be the lamb and not the wolf. But nowhere in the books did it tell Gubbio the truth: *You, citizens, will never actually be either.*

The wolf and the saint are more like one another than you are to either of them. For the hunger you know in yourselves, people of Gubbio, is not their hunger. Yours has no magic to it, and neither does your goodness. The beasts of your hunger and the saints of your righteousness will never leave your body to walk the highway together. Instead, they will remain, unbodied and uncertain, trapped inside your normal, human heart.

Outside yourself, past the city gates and beyond the amphitheater, the earth's Passionates might sometimes stand opposed, but they also twist into one another—swapping places, sharing legends. You, though, must only keep the news of them in your books. And in this, Brothers and Sisters, please take comfort.

Be thankful that your hunger is not capable of magic. It is a blessing to be lukewarm and full of prayers that don't wholly sustain you. So turn your heads from the window and go back to your fires, which are kept and modest. Labor inside the gates of your town and find the kingdom in your little picture books. Collect stones to build a church with high walls and towers and etch your saints and beasts over its doors. Pray safely inside that church for six hundred fifty years, and when the stones begin to give, do not let them molder like your old amphitheater. You must work many winters to refortify that holy church; rename it for your patron saint.

And when you unearth its foundation: Lo! You will find the bones of a wolf—or is it a dog?—buried beneath the stones.

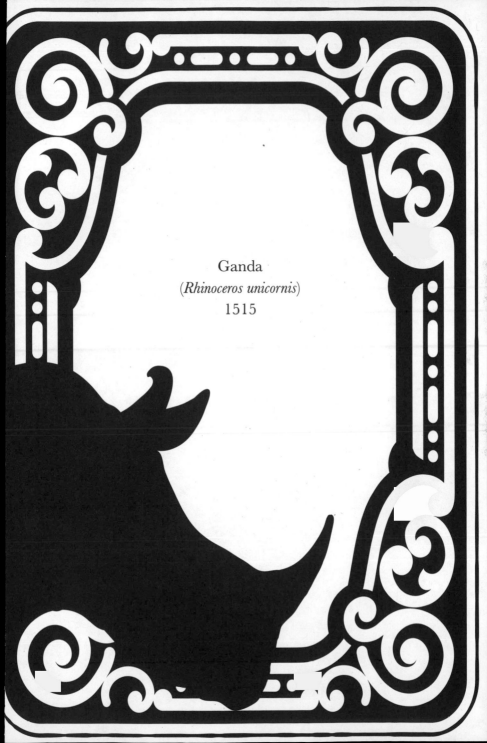

Ganda
(*Rhinoceros unicornis*)
1515

We know that this is a rhinoceros, even if it isn't.

Professor Evelyn Welch

ALBRECHT DÜRER NEVER SAW THE Monstrous Sow of Landser. Born on Suitbert's Feast Day in 1496, the pig lived for only twenty-four hours, on an edge of Germany far from Dürer's workshop. But news traveled faster than a body ever could, and by Easter, oddity-seekers all over the Empire had heard tell of the beast: a true *Doppelschwein*, with one head, two tongues, and no fewer legs than a spider.

Dürer probably did see Sebastian Brant's broadside when it made the Nuremberg rounds. Brant was near enough to go and view the *Schwein* while it lived, but the image it inspired in him was just a handful of thick, black strokes. In Brant's woodcut illustration, the pig's twin bellies touch and its four upper legs reach for their mates, as if courting a hug. Despite the two bodies converging in one head, it cuts a soft figure: more allemande than danse macabre.

Even from his 250-mile remove, Dürer knew he could get closer to an image that satisfied. It didn't matter that he lacked Brant's firsthand knowledge; a juicy picture could be sold as "drawn from the life" if the artist had only seen a dead and salted specimen or the crude sketches of an eyewitness's unsteady hand. Such was printmaking at the dawn of the Northern Renaissance, when half the world was built on hearsay, the rest on curiosity.

So Dürer reimagined his *Doppelschwein* as a sow and not a piglet—an adult monster for an adulterated world. And where Brant's woodcut is flat and simple, Dürer's copper intaglio hums with depth. The pig seems to fight a war inside itself. Caught midbleat, it kicks its useless top-hooves skyward. All six bottom legs stand hatched in kinetic shadow, and its two tails unravel in countering spirals. The basic porcine details are impeccable—bristling fur along its doubled back and a mouth wrenched open to reveal two dagger-tongues, each pointing to a different patch of Landser turf.

One print of Dürer's *Monstrous Sow* would sell in Nuremberg for the cost of a sausage: a pig for a pig. Or rather, a pig for the world. All around the Free City's markets—with their bratwursts and charms and broadsheet bestiaries—the shoppers sensed an anxious, almost giddy mutation in the open air. The city wasn't growing outward as much as all Creation was launching itself up and over the city gates, and each fresh discovery brought with it a retinue of unknowns, as well as new inventions.

Nuremberg had just seen its first globe and heard its first harpsichord. In 1510, the first pocket watch, called the "Nuremberg Egg," made time portable. And in the sixty-odd years since Gutenberg's press, six million books had made their way across Northern Europe, many of them starting in Nuremberg, the town with the largest paper mill. For the first moment in history, there were more pages on the continent than people: collectible battle maps, erotica, loose-leaf poems about the rock of fire that fell from Heaven to shake Ensisheim.

It was as if anything in your head could be confirmed by some far-flung report. Your wildest anxieties, your most Godforsaken imaginings—they could all be pulled out of the sky and made manifest in a woodcut of a nightmare beast, a fresh pox, or a folk-tale from the other side of a world that no longer *had* sides, as Magellan had just confirmed the Earth to be a deepening sphere.

In 1515, another broadside arrived at Dürer's workshop—not from Landser, but Lisbon. Some sultan had given the Portuguese king a nearly indescribable beast. It was a one-horned creature that fell beyond possibility, even in this century of the Landser sow and the double-necked Guggenheim goose. Unimaginable, even after the conjoined twins of Worms and the dog hatched from the egg of a bird.

The animal was last spotted in Europe centuries ago, in the ancient Colosseum, where it gutted panthers and bulls with its single horn and then fell asleep on the circus floor. The emperor Domitian had pressed its odd image into long-gone bronze coins. Pliny the Elder was so impressed with it that in the year 77, he declared the beast the king-elephant's natural rival, noting how, in a jungle battle, "it files that horn of his against hard stones" to stab the vulnerable pachyderm belly. But soon after that cameo in Pliny's *Naturalis Historia*, the horned animal disappeared from Europe altogether.

When it returned thirteen hundred years later, Portugal's King Manuel I remembered his Pliny. The spice ship bearing his living and breathing, two-ton gift docked in Lisbon's harbor and he quickly matched this new beast against the youngest elephant in his menagerie. The day of the fight, a Sumatran handler named Ocem hid the new creature, which he called Ganda, behind a giant arras in the Ribeira Palace courtyard. The elephant was decidedly less impressed by that big reveal than the crowd of clergymen, court artists, and nobles in attendance. It refused to even look upon Ganda's horn and stomped offstage without so much as a trumpet, Pliny be damned.

But imagine seeing Ganda's unthinkable form emerge from behind that tapestry. A creature you could never conjure on your own—bigger than the elephant, even!—with sectioned layers of dark grey hide, undertoned in pink, rippling over its skeleton like waves. What was a human mind to do with those comma-shaped ears and their distance from that squat, obscene horn? Who in Europe was prepared for those surprisingly small eyes fused to its cheeks, like mica bits in dirty marble? Not to mention the haunted way it rose to find its anger, seething rather than charging, as if the monster inside it just wanted to be left alone.

Among that Lisbon crowd was a printer—a German expat who still kept ties with tradesmen in Nuremberg. He sketched Ganda's hulking frame and giant horn, then wrote a description of the animal's qualities on a single sheet labeled RHINOCER-ON. He then forwarded the loose leaf north with a note: "On account of its wonderfulness, I thought myself obliged to send you a representation of it." And here, with this posted sketch, we see a creature split into two bodies.

The first body is exactly what Lisbon saw: Ganda's very skin, eye, and spike at the end of Ocem's tether. This is the body born in Sumatra and miraculously still alive after a four-month voyage to Portugal. After the failed fight, King Manuel will ship this body to Rome to test Pliny once again—this time in a bout with the Pope's white elephant, Hanno. This body will be wrapped for that voyage in green velvet and decked with carnations and gilt rope, perhaps to mimic wedding garb. The Ganda-body will make a pit stop to an island off Marseille so the king of France can wave at it from the shore. And two weeks afterward, that body will be chained to the bowels of the ship, still bound for Rome, when a storm sinks it to the bottom of the Ligurian Sea.

The second body is the one on the single page of the German printer's sketchbook—RHINOCERON—and it has so much further to travel. For RHINOCERON is not so much a body as it is the idea of one. RHINOCERON is a game of telephone, a centuries-long tumbling of names, shapes, misinterpretations, and forced significances. This idea of a body doesn't need chains or a spice ship or an Ocem to carry it. It is the horned body of paper. It wanders, unwarded, far from historical account and into a kind of shared continental dream.

This is a body born ages before King Manuel, when Emperor Domitian hammered the animal's crude image into his jubilee coin. And while the natural Ganda-body disappeared into the water, this body never left Europe. As it moved through the centuries—in books and in lore—it dragged along Pliny's claim of the elephant's enmity. The body appeared in the book of Job, renamed "behemoth," unfazed when the raging river Jordan flowed into its mouth. And in the medieval bestiaries, it somehow changed color; its horn grew sharper and went magical. Pliny's fighting beast, which he called "monoceron," then became the snow-white "unicorn" of the Middle Ages—a softer, godlier quadruped that man could only catch by using a virgin's lap as bait. A near millennium later, in *The Travels of Marco Polo*, it was called "nasty body," with a "pig-like head" burrowed in the Sumatran mud, "nothing like the unicorns of which our stories speak in Europe." You can almost see Marco Polo, years away from his homeland, shaking his head in confusion: "This creature is entirely different from what we fancied."

In 1515, these two bodies, the animal and the idea of an animal, ended up on the same continent. A *Doppelschwein* of natural fact and storytelling, set to spar. And after the little sketch labeled RHINOCERON made it up the courier road and into Nuremberg, the two bodies faced off in the mind of a forty-four-year-old printmaker with his very own press and near-limitless access to ink and paper and talent.

•• ▬ • ▬ ••

Albrecht Dürer had made his name on exactitude, especially when depicting living things. Look at the thousand-fold strands of water-color fur on his *Young Hare* or the perfect gouache feathers of his *Wing of a Blue Roller*. In *The Large Clump of Turf*, every reed and moss-curl has borne his scrutiny, down to the serration of each frond. Such precision turns the clump into the whole kingdom of Heaven, as marvelous as any monstrous sow. "Don't diverge from nature in your imaginings, thinking you want to find things for yourself," Dürer wrote. "In that way you will be led astray."

But throughout his body of work, Dürer took glorious pains to indulge his wayward imaginings, his dreams, and his borrowed truths. He was as quick to paint a Venetian crab as he was a sea monster carting a bored Milanese girl into the water. The same year as his *Clump of Turf* masterpiece, he illustrated one of his nightmares with a matter-of-fact calmness, as if it were a landscape out his window. In the margins of his notebook, he sketched a blood-red rain that supposedly fell on Nuremberg in 1503, dripping crucifix-shaped droplets onto the apron of his housemaid. Dürer, a clear product of his epoch, saw the internal and the external, the commonplace and the unknown, as facts of his planet.

A true artist, Dürer wrote, first masters the natural forms of the viewable world—fur, turf, wing—to fuel the more fanciful pockets of his art. One perfects the snout and the curly tail to earn the license to envision a vivid monstrous sow. Learning every ratio of a man, serpent, goat, and tiger lets one dream up an Apoca-lypse woodcut of a bishop falling into a dragon's mouth. And when a spotty sketch of something called RHINOCERON arrives one day in Nuremberg, these skills are what permits a master artist to fill in any gaps as he sees fit.

So this is what RHINOCERON is, according to Dürer. RHINOCERON is four stout legs and a head bowed low, facing left in a full suit of armor. RHINOCERON is a skeleton decked in seven fixed plates, each tessellated with its own scheme of sickles and ovoli. At the forearm and knee, these plates are seamed, like sleeves. And the sleeves have cuffs! A ring of dots, as if someone had pressed their thumb along the RHINOCERON like they would the crust of a pie. The butt has a topline of hook-and-eye loops, and the hip is a dead ringer for a tortoise shell. Its forehead is a line of thorns, its neck a collar of scallops.

In getting RHINOCERON onto the page, Dürer obviously borrowed from more familiar nature: hence the fuzzy sow's ears (much less oblong than Ganda's) and the paintbrush pony tail. Its scaled legs skew reptilian and its mouth is downright bovine. The nose-horn favors the unicorn's—long and somewhat thin, and straightened upward to a near-forty-five-degree angle. It pushes that horn against the borderline of the woodcut, as if nudging the door of a cage. And of course, according to Dürer, it sports that now-famous *extra* horn, sometimes called "the Dürer hornlette," which never appeared on a natural body. In the Dürer body, the hornlette sticks up—like a stiletto or a lifted pinky—at the nexus of the body's shoulders.

Why the extra horn? Why the gilded body armor? Was it misinformation—few know exactly what the RHINOCERON sketch from Lisbon told him—or was it Dürer's own wandering mind? No matter what, Dürer's animal image is both confounding and sticky. A new body presents itself at every glance; one viewing brings the familiarity of a low-eyed, four-footed beast, the next a still shot of a monster. Dürer has managed to represent both bodies—biological Ganda versus mythic RHINOCERON—and both realities—the natural versus the imagined—with a timeless artistry. To look at the animal body in that frame is to watch the weird and the comfortable in a battle royale. It produces a sensation not unlike that of pressing two magnets toward one another, poles aligned so that they shake.

"They call it a *Rhinocerus*," Dürer wrote at the top of the page. "It is represented here in its complete form."

A woodcut print could hit the Nuremberg market in less than a fortnight. After the artist made his master sketch, a *Formschneider* laid it over a thin block of pearwood. He'd gouge away all the blank space of the sketch by cutting against the wood grain with the most precise of blades, which caused the image to spring from the block in relief. After the block was rolled in ink and set to a heavy press, Dürer's *Rhinocerus* body would appear on a fresh page, shiny and black.

Once the paper was clipped on a line to dry, that same block could be immediately re-inked, and it was. At least four thousand times in Dürer's life, the workshop made a new *Rhinocerus*, and then again and again, long past his death in 1528. And further still into the 1600s, when the block changed hands and traveled to Holland. And again and again—as the border cracked, as worms ate away at the frame and at the scales of the legs, until the broken block could only manage a printing in green chiaroscuro.

Where only one Ganda-body was seen from ancient Rome to the Renaissance, thousands upon thousands of Dürer rhinos—extra horns and all—papered the continent in less than a century. And unlike the imagined RHINOCERON bodies of the myths or the bestiaries, which warped with every retelling, Dürer's *Rhinocerus* was legion and exact, its visible traits verbatim in every library and curiosity cabinet. It is difficult now to understand what that kind of exponential repetition, after so much nothing, did to a culture. Luckily, we've been left four centuries of visual evidence.

Natural histories and books of beasts in England, Belgium, and France began faithfully repeating the body as Dürer imagined it. Within a few decades, the Germans had nicknamed it *Panzernashorn*: a horn-and-armor. Travel books drew it—the plates, the sulk, the cow's lip—into places Ganda would never be seen, like China and the Cape of Good Hope. A Medici emblazoned the Dürer rhino on his crest, and France's Henry II ordered a wood totem of *Rhinocerus* trampling a lion for his royal parade. In 1580, a Habsburg archduke commissioned a portrait of a bride riding a *Rhinocerus* to her wedding. Italian sculptors chiseled its scowl into a Florentine grotto and a Sicilian fountain.

In the Flemish lowlands, ateliers hid the Dürer body in the glorious leaves of their tapestries—boarding the Ark or grimacing alongside a warbling Orpheus. The bodies always struck the same pose as that of the print: facing the same direction, the head down and the face stoic, a little bored. The same year Vermeer painted his shimmering, perfect *Lacemaker*, Francis Barlow drew the *Rhinocerus* stabbing an elephant in the gut, just as Pliny intended. Also that year, a man in Persia sketched a body that much more closely resembled Ganda's, but no one in Europe noticed.

Parisian weavers stitched two *Rhinocerus* yoked at the shoulder-horns, glumly pulling a battle chariot. Eighty years after that, the same looms wove a scene of the hornletted body watching a cheetah gnaw at a zebra's neck. That gory scene was reproduced again and again for five decades, until the weaving cartoons dissolved. And on and on, with nothing in the real world to fact-check it, into the eighteenth century, when it was inlaid on card tables and carved into tortoiseshell chessboards and onyx cameos. These reproductions were never Dürer-perfect—proportions changed, as did color and skill—but the shoulder plates and swirly hornlette and *Rhinocerus* glower were there. Within two centuries, a hundred thousand specimens of a creature, until nearly anyone could name

the body on sight. *Dies ist ein wunderbares Panzernashorn!*—caged in
oil or thread or porcelain, on platters, vases, urns, or goblets too
fancy to drink from.

••▬•▬••

It took 226 years for *Rhinocerus* to meet a flesh-and-blood opponent. A docile female body, "tame as a lambe," she toured Europe throughout the middle of the eighteenth century in a wagon
drawn by twenty horses. Crowds from Copenhagen to Naples paid
a pittance to walk by her. Some spent more to sit on bleachers and
watch her eat hay, and a few "persons of rank" paid to ride on her
back. Her charges must have noticed, once they straddled her, the
way her flesh heaped over itself, rather than locking into place, and
the lack of a horn twirling up from her withers.

No Ganda-bodied beast had traveled this much of the continent, or managed to stay alive on it for so long. She caused a panic.
They called her Clara.

And here, in 1749, is where the 1515 Ganda tale almost re-
peats. King Louis XV's "Painter of the Hunt" went to Versailles to
sketch something alive and wonderful. But unlike the artist in the
Lisbon palace two centuries before him, this man, named Oudry,
studied Clara's body for days, perhaps longer if he followed her
to her summer stint in Paris. Oudry made not one, but several
images—some in red chalk, others on blue paper—all drawn from
the life sat before him.

One image was sent to a French illustrator, who copied it for a
blockbuster encyclopedia. Unlike Dürer, this artist kept his imagination in check, and so it is very much a Clara-body that appears
in those thousands of copies of the *Histoire Naturelle*. The book
moved so quickly its publishers were forced to rush-order a second
printing within six weeks. This is how Clara's body—the Ganda

body—became one that a child could pick out of a lesson book or draw from memory. Europe saw her not as a myth, but as a creature that might be the next town over, like a sow or a young hare. The year of her death, 242 years after Ganda's, Linnaeus named her *Rhinoceros unicornis*. And a new figure began making appearances on the wool rugs and porcelain urns, with its darker skin, its single horn, and its friendlier mouth opened as if to bite leaf from limb. Oudry debuted a fifteen-foot-long oil of her in a salon of the Louvre, naming the painting in the Linneaen fashion—*Rhinoceros*.

On the gigantic canvas, Clara shows her right side with her head up and her ears pricked. Her skinfolds have the pink shadow we now know comes natural to her kind. Rather than armed for battle, she looks wet and almost sleek. Her eye is a foreign black bead enclosed in red.

Despite the keen likeness it strikes, something about the giant portrait falls flat. Though deeply aware of proportion, coloring, and posture, *Rhinoceros* is static, as if it refuses to open itself. Nothing has morphed; nothing is out of place. Nothing inside the body fights to escape.

Oudry's *Rhinoceros* amplifies a basic limitation: the barrier that a natural animal body presents to human understanding. We humans can only go so far toward another "real" creature. An artist who opts to replicate exactly what a human can see when he stands before an animal can't help but create this deficit. Something disappears when we bear witness to nature with such gorgeous accuracy. This disappearance isn't only in painting. Even if Clara arrived in our town, even if we paid the extra shillings to touch her, the space between the flesh of our palms and the other side of her dark body would be vast and absolute.

For what Nuremberger knows how a young hare sees the world? Who in Landser comprehends what time means to a sow, monstrous or otherwise? And, perhaps even more importantly, what on earth is a European really looking at when his eye falls upon a two-ton beast from Assam? At Versailles, on the Ribeira Palace courtyard, or in any *parc sauvage* that stands a four-month journey from Ganda's rightful corner of the planet, what are we really looking at? Her body reminds us of this distance. It reminds us that a specimen like Clara—raised indoors since birth, barreling from country to country in a cage so tight she rubs away her own horn on the walls—might always feel more dreamed-up than a woodcut print on a Nuremberg wall.

What's absent from Oudry's magnificent *Rhinoceros* painting? Misinformation. Perhaps what made Dürer's take on the beast so repeatable, so *close* to us, is that a rhinoceros never stood before him. If the live animal body serves as a boundary, then the missing body allowed Dürer to step into that ancient RHINOCERON and sketch it from the inside out. And under the skin, he placed another animal entirely. It could be that all we really see when we look at a *Rhinocerus* print (as we now have for a half millennium) is an interior—one that's made of what *we* wonder, what *we* want, and what confuses *us*. Not the facts of a rhinoceros, but a two-horned body twisted by the facts of human anxiety and awe.

Dürer's *Rhinocerus* depicts the art of living in a modern world that can import gigantic creatures that we'll never fully understand. *Rhinocerus* depicts the unnatural reality of being *Homo sapiens* in a modern world this monstrous, this unknowable, and this full of utter nonsense. The rhinoceros and the idea of a rhinoceros. Dürer's trick was to harness the loaded moment in which human imagination—destructive, mutative, and tricky—fights the realities of our planet and, real or not, bests them.

Perhaps this besting is why in 1745, amid all the Clara fever, a sulking, incorrect figure appeared on the Duke of Northumberland's servingware. Its superfluous hornlette pointed to the top of the plate like a middle finger. A decade later, Dürer's

Rhinocerus walked across the lids of delicate piqué snuffboxes. When rococo animal clocks were all the rage, master craftsman Jean-Joseph de Saint-Germain offered a one-horned Clara clock case, but he also sold a hornletted *Rhinocerus* model for his more traditional patrons.

Again and again, into the nineteenth century, even though five more *Rhinoceros unicornis* had visited the continent by then, "Dürer's rhino" still hung on Europe's walls. The British Museum acquired Dürer's original drawing in 1895, and they still keep it in the museum's print vault as "the great popular image of European art." Victorian critic James Bruce called it "wonderfully ill-executed in all its parts" and named Dürer "the origin of all the monstrous forms under which that animal has been painted ever since."

The Wonderful and the Monstrous: such are the twists of the *Rhinocerus* helix. This is what it means to be a creature whose native habitat is human thought.

This is what makes Nandalal Bose, born in 1882 and called "the Dürer of modern Indian art," sketch a bold linocut of a Dürer *Rhinocerus* body for a Bengali storybook.

This is what led to Bernhard Jager's inside-out, Dürer-posed lithograph, *(interior workings of a Rhinoceros)*, seventy years later.

This is what kept a wrong-bodied *Panzernashorn* in German schoolbooks past the First World War.

And this is what made Salvador Dalí never forget the *Rhinocerus* print that hung in his boyhood home. Four decades into adulthood, Dalí announced he was "becoming classical" in order to keep fighting for irrational discoveries. He finagled an invite to the Louvre so he could copy Vermeer's classic *The Lacemaker* in a back room. Less than an hour into the session, he looked at his canvas and found he'd instead painted three rhino horns crashing into each other. In the spirals of the horns, Dalí said he discovered "a violent force" atomic to all art. Every European painting was, he said, at its heart, a rhinoceros.

Now what else could Dalí do but spend the next decade painting rhinoceroses, from the inside out? He adopted Dürer's *Rhinocerus* as a personal emblem, just as that Medici did four hundred years earlier, and then he painted his wife Gala as the Virgin, her bones dissolving into white horn-splinters. In 1954, he reimagined a portrait of a nude at a window "auto-sodomized by the [rhino] horns of her own chastity." The next year, he painted a "paranoiac-critical" study of the Vermeer as an explosion of cylindrical horns. And one year later, he sculpted a Dürer *Cosmic Rhinoceros* in bronze with spider-legs and a third, gold horn way too long to be just a hornlette. It twists above the center of the rhino's back and doubles the sculpture's height.

And what better pièce de résistance could Dalí have dreamt than the day he burst into the rhino enclosure of the Vincennes zoo with a film crew hot on his tail? There, Dalí set up an easel near the zoo's resident Ganda-body, named François. In the film crew's silent footage, the animal paces behind Dalí, who holds his thumb to a copy of Vermeer's delicate *Lacemaker* on an easel. After an assistant places a conical hunk of bread—a makeshift horn—to an incorrect spot on Dalí's scalp, the film cuts to a new location. Dalí has dangled a huge print of *The Lacemaker* over the mouth of the rhino's cave: another challenge between a body of nature and a body of art.

The rhinoceros approaches Vermeer's painting, seems to sniff it, then bows its head. Low and vulnerable, it backs away in a series of stutter-steps before turning in a circle and walking out of the frame. Then another cut: after picking up a long, thin horn and holding it perpendicular to his body, like a jousting sword, Dalí charges the *Lacemaker* print himself—runs his body right through it; the natural rhino is nowhere in sight. Though the film is silent, you can almost hear the artist hollering as the giant paper rips to pieces, shouting what he said to his wife the first time he ever held a piece of the beast in his hands: "THIS HORN WILL SAVE MY LIFE!"

Sackerson
(*Ursus arctos*)
1601

I have seen Sackerson loose twenty times, and have taken him by the
chain; but, I warrant you, the women have so cried and shrieked at it,
that it passed.

Slender, *The Merry Wives of Windsor*

THE LONDON GARDEN, BRACKISH AND packed-in, was hazy with a dozen kinds of flesh. The bulls, cocks, mastiffs, men, and chimpanzees in air so rickety it lowered the roof. So dark, the line 'tween crowd and beasts was marred. There, in that black, Sir Raleigh took his Frenchmen, and other men of duty met their spies. The reason for the famous fireworks? Just so the folks who'd wagered bets could see.

A rose of flames, pitched high above the crowd, fired smoke into the muck that hung about. It spun and spat red bits around the seats. They'd rigged it to throw pears as it rotated; the fruit-mad crowd would then jump up and chase the rolling pears out to the Bankside streets. Or yardboys, eager in their dirty gloves, would toss hot bread upon the patrons' laps, which made them clutch and scurry toward the exit. Outside, they'd find some other Sunday sport: an arch'ry butt, a woman, or a play.

The stews downriver had less fornication. And St. Barthol'mew's floors less wet with blood. The bloody muzzle or the mastiff's blood. The blood from fisticuffs up in the stands. The blood of offal, floated down the Thames to Bankside from the abattoirs of town. And by the time the century turned around, it seemed the blood most often spilled was his.

But do not think that London's garden crowd imagined him a broken, bashed-in thing. Believe me, this is tricky. I might see the lives of baited bears as nothing but a broken chord of muzzle, chain, and stake. Of blunted teeth, barrages of dog jaws, of living-out a mongrel just to have another thrown upon the slavered flesh. That rink's the only place that he could run, a hard-won constitutional—fighting dogs and running laps in that dank polygon. That garden, broken even in its flowers—the rosettes they affixéd to his brow were bull's-eyes for the mastiffs when they jumped. And jump they did, mouths tearing up the flesh that leered at them from each side of the bloom. They bit so hard that London's citizens grew up thinking a bear's eyes to be pink.

Few years of that, he was too blind to fight; the bearwards had to get creative then. Chained center, hunkered, lashed by volunteers until the blood ran rivers down his spine. Sometimes he'd raise his matted arms and gnash about the lash until it broke in half. And once, he stooped low to the lazy knot, untied himself with effort from the stake, and nosed about the rink in backward loops to hear the ladies scream, the bearwards scramble. They dragged him off-stage to his pit in cheers.

For even then, near-lame and sightless, he could still throw nine-stone mastiffs to the stands. Up to the boxes, to the ladies' laps, bypassing pumpkin hose, straight to the skirts. Like he could sniff a woman's quivering thigh and hurl the big dog, head o'er tail, right to her. A snort, a twitch to shudder the dog spit, a fling, a lady's lap

a-going *oof!* And then they'd add another dog, then two . . . till six
or seven mastiffs lined the rink, the sound more deafening since his
sight was gone. Goddammit if he wasn't still around. They could
have put his picture on the money.

Elizabeth, who never said hullo, loved him enough to ban all
Thursday sport. Upon the mildest Thursdays, he'd parade out past
the playhouse, down to London Bridge. He'd smell the ragmen,
actors, punks in stews who yelled for him in ripe cacophony. The
bulls, in ribboned horns, all marched behind; the cocks-in-boxes
and the dogs behind. The Only Bear That Ever Led the Dogs.

And even on his nights off, he appeared: in name-checks at the
Hope, the Rose, the Globe. A dactyl in the mouths of water poets.
The only rival Shakespeare called by name. In Jonson. In act
five at Dunsinane. At Middle Temple Hall on Candlemas, when
Chamber's fairest boy-in-fake-dugs crooned: *Have you not set mine
honor at the stake / and baited it with all th'unmuzzled thoughts / that tyran-
nous heart can think?*

So. It'd be wrong to match that bear with breaking; they built him
up. They called him out by name because they read in him a secret
code both terrifying and recognizable. They saw it in his stance—
up on two legs, the forepaws spread, the ten claws digital. They
saw it in his low-slung hips and gut. The way his pupils, round and
beady, lived inside a circle of expressive white. And milliseconds
prior to the bite, they saw it as he bowed his head and sighed.

What did they see? They saw themselves, of course.

A taller man—more leaden and hirsute, with thick skin better
suited for a beating, but still their bear. This massive chestnut

frame, dwarfed tiny by a darkened ring of foes. A smaller ratio of the rink itself, dwarfed by the river flowing to its north: that lurid, pestilent Thames. Six city plagues—the pox, the "new ague," the curious "sweats"—all floated past the bear garden in leagues. A river of unprecedented sick. In '92 things got so royally poxed, the playhouses were forced to shutter up. A quarter of their population down each decade, give or take a hundred score.

A blighted age can make a garden blind. Each ticketholder turns left, right, behind, and wonders which part of their dark quartet will suffer an unnatural upset next. For when our clans explode up into towns, the back-bite comes from nature, and it *smarts*. The devil holds back nature by its ears, takes aim, makes wager, then releases it. We toss it off and it regenerates; six natural mouths leap forth before we're primed.

Parades of sickness cannot be explained by any learnéd clansmen: physics, priests. The inexplicable can send us toward an unclanned occupation with the self. And selves, like famous bears, are singular. "We are" soon switches places with "I am." Then clans bewitched by "I ams" become crowds, which are an altogether different thing. He heard those iams in the garden's roar:

I am this bear, stuck in this blighted rink, beset upon by nature's ticking clock. I am not hunkered down in numbered packs; instead I am awaiting death alone. I am afraid of time's encroaching power, for each new year, I am more bluntly struck. I feel pain, feel it doubling, then I am it; I am always in wait of time's new teeth. And though befuddled, drunk on sick, I am unfit to tear my eyes away from *him*.

The growl of him, his mighty swipe, his blood, the way he foams both in and out of hours. My chain of foes would weigh less, I am sure, if I could toss off minutes, break pain's spine, or send plague—squealing—to a bitch's lap. For even if I knew more time, more sick, was at the go, it'd be a righteous salve to fight whatever hour's on me now. To discard the sick dog of what is now. To throw it—a contaminated rag stained with the gusto of my intellect.

Yes. I am jealous of his natural acts. And so I'll hit his nature with a stick.

Jeoffry
(*Felis catus*)
1760

> 68 Let SHEPHATIAH rejoice with the little Owl, which is the winged Cat.
> 68 For I am possessed of a cat, surpassing in beauty, from whom I take occasion to bless Almighty God.
>
> Christopher Smart, *Jubilate Agno*, Fragment B

695 Let the UNNAMED CAT of Cyprus consider the man in its tomb.

696 Let SEKHMET uncover the straggled with a sandy cat's-breath.

697 Let TA-MIU keep the crown prince a-catted 'til dawn.

698 Let LOMASA, trapped in the doxy net, take pains to skirt his struggles.

699 Let BASTET's temple rise catastrophic.

700 Let GOTOKU-JI's Holy-Cat snuff the pilgrim's fire.

701 Let OVINNIK chase ghosts from frenzïed SMARTS.

702 Let all menagerie cats praise tenfold their JEOFFRY!

703 Let the Ocelot give her singular kit for Jeoffry to embrace.

704 Let the Lion sneeze as he did on the Ark and bring forth double Jeoffrys.

705 Let the Panther slumber three days past Jeoffry's rollicks.

706 Let the Wildcat quarter his killing and share it.

707 Let the Jaguar's quintessence refute all the filth.

708 Let the Pard teach Jeoffry six ways of escapement.

695 *For I will consider my Cat Jeoffry.*

696 *For he is the servant of the Living God duly and daily serving him.*

697 *For at the first glance of the glory of God in the East he worships in his way.*

698 *For this is done by wreathing his body seven times round with elegant quickness.*

699 *For then he leaps up to catch the musk, which is the blessing of God upon his prayer.*

700 *For he rolls upon prank to work it in.*

701 *For having done duty and received blessing he begins to consider himself.*

702 *For this he performs in ten degrees.*

703 *For first he looks upon his fore paws to see if they are clean.*

704 *For secondly he kicks up behind to clear away there.*

705 *For thirdly he works it upon stretch with the fore paws extended.*

706 *For fourthly he sharpens his paws by wood.*

707 *For fifthly he washes himself.*

708 *For Sixthly he rolls upon wash.*

709 Let the Catamount hide the bite half a fortnight.

710 Let the Lynx rejoice—up, down, sideways infinitum.

711 Let the Cheetah run Jeoffry nine quick miles from LOGIC.

712 Let the Lion mark J with an uproarious X.

713 Let all marbled thinkers keep Cats near their books.

714 Let JOHNSON enshrine good HODGE in his study.

715 Let MONTAIGNE cat-sport with Mme. VANITY (or does she man-sport with him)?

716 Let JEROME be-saint the Cat who stalks his papers for the murine.

717 Let SCARLATTI give his PULCINELLA a jaunty left-hand line.

718 Let not PANGUR BÀN disappear his kept monk with unseeing.

719 Let RICHELIEU's bed-lamps alight on LUDOVIC.

720 Let WALPOLE mourn poor SELIMA, murdered by goldfish.

721 Let all kept creatures bask in the light of the one true MAGNIFICAT!

722 Let Jeoffry rebuff any traffic with a suspect stripe.

723 Let his man not be called mad, though he shows his Tiger teeth.

724 Let Jeoffry not live as a May-cat (one a-kept by melancholia).

725 Let trouble befall those who expectorate Cat slander.

709 For Seventhly he fleas himself, that he may not be interrupted upon the beat.

710 For Eighthly he rubs himself against a post.

711 For Ninthly he looks up for his instructions.

712 For Tenthly he goes in quest of food.

713 For having consider'd God and himself he will consider his neighbour.

714 For if he meets another cat he will kiss her in kindness.

715 For when he takes his prey he plays with it to give it chance.

716 For one mouse in seven escapes by his dallying.

717 For when his day's work is done his business more properly begins.

718 For he keeps the Lord's watch in the night against the adversary.

719 For he counteracts the powers of darkness by his electrical skin and glaring eyes.

720 For he counteracts the Devil, who is death, by brisking about the life.

721 For in his morning orisons he loves the sun and the sun loves him.

722 For he is of the tribe of Tiger.

723 For the Cherub Cat is a term of the Angel Tiger.

724 For he has the subtlety and hissing of a serpent, which in goodness he suppresses.

725 For he will not do destruction, if he is well-fed, neither will he spit without provocation.

726 Let the washerfrau who beats the cat besoak her own damned line.

727 Let HOGARTH's wanton boys, who string up tails, meet the sticks.

728 Let Jeoffry not catch curses on a Scottish belvedere.

729 Let J not shield the soldier-breast at the gates to Pelusium.

730 Let all SMARTS keep Cats as kin, as each Kit must be kept.

731 Let all hounds bring unto Jeoffry the continental praise.

732 Let hounds be known as mirrors of men, but Cats? A tidy-foot beyond them.

733 Let JEOFFRY reflect neither God nor man, but a set of dogged peculiars.

734 Let Jeoffry be given the hound bone, the tooth, and the scratch.

735 Let the stale ideas of all your hounds heretoforely be doggerel.

736 Let Jeoffry tread forward with gusto.

737 Let his gait be unchecked and undogly.

738 Let it be known that the space between God and SMART men is prayer.

739 Let it be known that prayer moves man and God into fragmentary bits.

740 Let it be known that fragmented prayer is heard in the cat's nipping cry.

741 Let it be known: there's no sickness darker than bridging two fragments with LOGIC.

742 Let the two fragments—godly and Smartly—rejoin with a *Cat'i'th'gap!*

726 For he purrs in thankfulness, when God tells him he's a good Cat.

727 For he is an instrument for the children to learn benevolence upon.

728 For every house is incompleat without him and a blessing is lacking in the spirit.

729 For the Lord commanded Moses concerning the cats at the departure of the
      Children of Israel from Egypt.
730 For every family had one cat at least in the bag.

731 For the English Cats are the best in Europe.

732 For he is the cleanest in the use of his fore-paws of any quadrupede.

733 For the dexterity of his defence is an instance of the love of God to him
      exceedingly.
734 For he is the quickest to his mark of any creature.

735 For he is tenacious of his point.

736 For he is a mixture of gravity and waggery.

737 For he knows that God is his Saviour.

738 For there is nothing sweeter than his peace when at rest.

739 For there is nothing brisker than his life when in motion.

740 For he is of the Lord's poor and so indeed is he called by benevolence perpetually—
      Poor Jeoffry! poor Jeoffry! the rat has bit thy throat.
741 For I bless the name of the Lord Jesus that Jeoffry is better.

742 For the divine spirit comes about his body to sustain it in compleat cat.

743 Let cat-particulars keep odd time and vociferate all hours.

744 Let cat-thoughts keep a human body sweetly outside itself.

745 Let cattery soothe the kept man, be he a-bed, at-desk, or exiled.

746 Let the *vox felis* remind us: days at a desk *are* a kind of a keeping.

747 Let the kept Man-at-desk worship the Cat like a leaping Byzantine.

748 Let the Man-at-desk go a-catting to squelch the roll and the prank of his mind.

749 Let Cat pranks parcel out into WAGGLES, for the Man-at-desk's delighting.

750 Let the Cat-waggle-visions pass desk-to-desk and man-to-man, as do the Ballads.

751 Let Cat-waggle-tales alight on the desks of all those kept by drudgery.

752 Let Cat-waggle-ditties goose the clock of the jeopardized and bedrugged.

753 Let the Cat-waggles invade continent and colonies.

754 Let God bless the SMART who sends a J-waggle down the hump!

755 Let Cat-waggle-dreams solve all desky jeopardies, and to the letter.

756 Let J be the missing form—bless those who fly their keep at first watch!

757 Let E be the eye of Jeoffry, and the eye that disremembers all I's.

758 Let O be the illogic that circles in vigilance, like a Cat near sleep.

759 Let F be *Felidae Felis*, which—O HOLY CATS!—is doubly fine.

760 Let R be not what we are, but what we err, and whate'er strikes us.

743 For his tongue is exceeding pure so that it has in purity what it wants in musick.

744 For he is docile and can learn certain things.

745 For he can set up with gravity, which is patience upon approbation.

746 For he can fetch and carry, which is patience in employment.

747 For he can jump over a stick which is patience upon proof positive.

748 For he can spraggle upon waggle at the word of command.

749 For he can jump from an eminence into his master's bosom.

750 For he can catch the cork and toss it again.

751 For he is hated by the hypocrite and miser.

752 For the former is afraid of detection.

753 For the latter refuses the charge.

754 For he camels his back to bear the first notion of business.

755 For he is good to think on, if a man would express himself neatly.

756 For he made a great figure in Egypt for his signal services.

757 For he killed the Ichneumon-rat very pernicious by land.

758 For his ears are so acute that they sting again.

759 For from this proceeds the passing quickness of his attention.

760 For by stroaking of him I have found out electricity.

761 Let Y be YES; two short roads to a line, which is why, Jeoffry? And
    then yes, Jeoffry.

762 Let 74 lines of Cat-letting meet 74 lines of warm, for-wanting love.

763 Let a line of Cats waggling against the ceaseless prayer be love.

764 Let Jeoffry hover over the road and then let his low roving be love.

765 Let his feet pad the road and find a man, kneeling a-fours, for love.

766 Let his cat-jig, cat-bourrée and cat-Sarabande be-spraggle us as love.

767 Let a Cat to a drowning man be love.

768 Let love be his keep.

—for Alexi Morrissey

761 *For I perceived God's light about him both wax and fire.*

762 *For the Electrical fire is the spiritual substance, which God sends from heaven to sustain the bodies both of man and beast.*
763 *For God has blessed him in the variety of his movements.*

764 *For, tho' he cannot fly, he is an excellent clamberer.*

765 *For his motions upon the face of the earth are more than any other quadrupede.*

766 *For he can tread to all the measures upon the musick.*

767 *For he can swim for life.*

768 *For he can creep.*

Vogel Staar
(*Sturnus vulgaris*)
1784

He was not naughty, quite,
But gay and bright.
And under all his brag,
A foolish wag.
W.A. Mozart

WHISTLE A LITTLE MOZART TO a starling in a cage. If it knows humans as creatures that sing and are sung to, the bird will shut its beak. It will arch its starling neck, bending toward your puckered lips. It might bob its dark head back and forth at the Mozart line you've sent out—the dotted pops of "Papageno, Papagena" or the crystalline shards of the Rondo for Glass Harmonica. Though a caged starling is chatty during the day and downright garrulous at night, at the moment it locks in on your Mozartean whistle, the little bird will only blink, aiming its entire soundless self toward the music coming from you. Note how it nods along with your tuneful body as if to say, *Yes, yes, I have it.*

But a starling is no parrot. Do not expect that when you whistle "twin-kle, twin-kle," you'll immediately hear a "lit-tle star" in return. You'll have to come back whistling for a day or a week, confirming the sound's place in the world where the bird perches. And when it does spit back whatever Mozart you've fed it, it will be on a starling's zany terms: a theme from the "Haffner" symphony punctuated with guttural warbles, or the famous Adagio from his Clarinet Concerto mixed into an uncanny impression of your dishwasher. The "Queen of the Night" aria sung in a screech worthy of a Bee Gee.

A few days after that, your line of Mozart will come from the birdcage as a barely recognizable string of filched sounds, all sung together in a line so arrhythmic, it's catchy. You'll hear Mozart, your own voice, the white noise of the house you live in, plus the recesses of starling instinct:

> TWIN-KLE—*bizeeet!*—TWIN—*"hi! how are you!"*—
> *[doorbell]*—KLE—*chackerchackerchacker*—LIT-TLE—
> *bweet!bweet!purrrup!*—LIT-TLE—*[cranging smoke alarm]*—
> LIT—*"hi!how are you"*—TLE, TWIN-KLE, LIT-TLE—
> *[that Bee Gees screech]*——STAAAAAAR!

This will then be repeated with the maddening obsessiveness of an electronica concert.

We're not sure why starlings engage in such behavior, but we think it's because this breed is hardwired to sing to its tribes. There are many in a starling's life: the little tribe of the monogamous pair, that of the clutch family, the flock in the field, the mob coming home from the neighboring fields to roost together overnight. All these tribes are sonic. The male starling sings his long coupling song to his mate while she pecks for food. A young starling sends mad chatter to her close-by kin to feel where the safe world starts and stops. A wizened starling finds his place in the mob by singing long runs of mashed-up noise that prove his vast experience.

This sonic sense of the tribal might explain why, when we see a trilling mob of ten thousand starlings—each bird watching its seven closest neighbors for the slightest change of speed or angle, dodging hawks en masse with shrieks and chips, beak beats and hard whistles—we find ourselves calling that group not a flock or a swarm or a drove, but a collective noun that's drenched in sound: a "murmuration."

So what kind of murmur began that spring day in Vienna when a twenty-eight-year-old Mozart, jaunty in his garnet coat and gold-rimmed cap, strolled into a shop to whistle at a starling in a cage? That bird must have zeroed in on Mozart's mouth as the man whistled the seventeen-note opening phrase from his recent piano concerto:

Mozart's melody riffs in G on a simple line heard in many a *Volkslied*, so the starling might have been hearing similar tunes from other shoppers that whole month. Or perhaps Mozart himself had been in a few times and had whistled his line enough for the bird to learn it. No matter how the starling got the song, on May 27, 1784, it spat that tune right back at the tunesmith—but not without taking some liberties first.

The little songbird unslurred the quarter notes and added a dramatic fermata at the end of the first full measure; we can only guess how long it held that warbly G. At the next bar, it lengthened Mozart's staccato attack and replaced his effete grace notes with two pairs of bold crotchets. And the starling had the audacity to sharp the two Gs of the second measure, when any Viennese composer worth his wig would keep them natural and in line with the key. Those bird-born G-sharps take the steady folk tune into a more harmonically complex place, ignoring the fermata-ed natural G of the earlier measure and pushing toward the next note in the phrase—an A—which builds a lifted E-major chord instead.

Mozart apparently loved this edit, because he bought that bird on sight. For good measure, he drew a little treble staff in his expense book and scored the starling's tweaks under the note of purchase:

Vogel Staar, 34 Kreutzer:

And under the last measure: an acclamation scribbled in the maestro's quick hand: *Das war schön!*

There is no other live animal purchase in Mozart's expense book, and no more handwritten melodies; no additional transactions were praised as *schön!* This is one of the very few things we even know about his purchasing habits. He'd only begun tracking his spending that year, and by late summer, Mozart had abandoned the practice and only used that notebook to magpie random phrases of English. So this note of purchase is special among the extant scraps from his life.

He also bought the bird at a critical point for the Classical period. At the end of the eighteenth century, tunes were never more sparkling or more kept, their composers obsessive over the rhetoric of sonata form: first establishing a theme, then creating tension through a new theme and key, then stretching it into a dizzying search for resolution, and finally finding the resolve in a rollicking coda. The formal understanding of this four-part structure permeated Classical symphony, sonata, and concerto. By 1784, sonata form had imprinted itself on the listening culture enough to feel like instinct; Vienna audiences could rest comfortably in the run of Classical forms as familiar—and thus enjoyable—narratives. And nobody played this cagey game more giddily than Mozart.

Of all the things Johann Chrysostom Wolfgang Amadeus Mozart brought to human sound, the most important might be his sense of surprise. His compositions, while almost always law-abiding, are full of trickery—leading tones that drop away from roots, accidentals that jar the listening mind from its diverted stupor, minuets too syncopated to dance to. His beloved Piano Concerto in D Minor begins not with a sturdy melody, but an anti-tune of the same repeated notes bouncing about the orchestra. Songs from his early operas confounded audiences with their false endings. He reveled in keys like A minor, with its air of turmoil and instability.

These caprices, though stuck inside the pinfold of common practice, are what made him a star. As the old German saying goes, the music of Bach gave us God's word, Beethoven's gave us God's fire, but Mozart's gave God's laughter to the world. He found the accidents in song that reminded music to glorify the playful, the mischievous, the *pop!* that sends Jack exploding from the box after so much measured cranking.

So the starling's playful G-sharp must have felt more than *schön* to the maestro, and worth more to him than thirty-four damn kreutzer. Think of it—he'd whistled a tune steeped in Vienna's golden algebra to a thing with feathers, and then the animal bobbed its little head and whistled back to him a glorious, deviant, Mozartean wink. This wasn't just *schön*; it was game recognizing game! It's difficult to imagine a more priceless moment: one of the greatest thinkers in history bonding with a bird brain.

We still know very little about the starling brain, really. Our science is just catching up to the species's complex body and behavior, some 225 years after Mozart's death. Among our recent discoveries is a sturdy musical form inside one type of starling song. Though the structure allows enough variation for one starling to sound nothing like the next bird over, all courting males organize their love songs into a four-part sequence of whistle, warble, click, and screech.

Each bird begins with a set of repeated whistles—a kind of reedy introduction. Next, as the feathers at his throat seethe and puff, he weaves a run of maddening musical snippets—as few as ten or as many as thirty-five—curated into descending tones. Some of these snippets are filched from nearby species (or lawn equipment, or cellular phones). It's here, in this second movement, that the "twin-kle, twin-kle" meets the *chackerchacker*, the smoke alarm, and the Bee Gees. Without stopping, he then slams into the third section, that of the percussive click solo. Syncopated and noteless rattles shoot from his beak at *presto* speed, as many as fifteen clicks per second. And then he ends with a *fortissimo* finale of loud, exclamatory shrieks—enough to wake the neighbors.

It can take him a full minute to sing through all four movements, and then the starling is silent for a moment. Some birds even bow when they've finished.

Nearly every courting male in the wild follows this pattern. The four movements are audible even to human ears if we listen closely enough. Because a bird can log so many random sounds in his song bank, the permutations of starling form are endless. And unlike the work of Mozart and company, there is no discernable meter, math, or key dictating the starling's changes from the whistle movement to the warble movement or from click to screech. The bird can do what it wants in each section for as long as it likes. This gives the courted female two distinct pleasures: she can lean on the familiarity of the song structure, but she can also hear the freestyle within the movement—a report of her lover's unique mind.

Because of its tendency to absorb sound, the starling's song is not tuneful as much as it is expansive. The world spills into its music; the real meets the obsessive, the merry smashes into the flatulent. The compositions of this species are joyful and ugly and dissonant and divine. And though less predictable than the whippoorwill's or the skylark's, the starling's song is by no means less confident.

Though we know this much about starling composition, the mental process that cultivates these choices—whatever gray matter lets a starling write its own song and wills it to vary its tunes—remains mysterious. After a millennium of searching, we cannot figure out where in the brain this starling song is bred. It's possible the whole process is the result of a mental function humans simply don't possess. Or most of us don't, anyway.

Mozart's brain is as much a mystery as a starling's. It was never autopsied and his genetic line ended with his two surviving children. In 1801, a gravedigger claimed he'd unearthed Mozart's skull, but no one has been able to prove it. We've simply spent the past two hundred years guessing what went on in Mozart's head, and as long as we keep his six-hundred-plus compositions in heavy rotation, we'll always have half a mind to try to figure him out. His music's heavy presence in our lives, from "Twinkle, Twinkle" to the Requiem, keeps us guessing.

The old ideas of Mozart as a perpetual child or as a mere recipient of dictation from God have dissolved in recent years, thanks to computer studies of his "autograph scores" that show revision after revision scribbled onto the pages in multiple inks. We now know Mozart drafted and woodshedded for his entire career. He didn't simply spit music out; musical ideas incubated inside him for decades.

Despite our better understanding of the scope of his efforts, it's difficult to ignore the flighty irreverence he possessed, both on and off the staff. Many have wondered why a brain that prone to perfection was so hell-bent on vandalism. Mozart loved to chatter, play, and shock. Who, for example, could imagine Bach or Beethoven jumping out of his chair at a performance, as Mozart did, and somersaulting around while the soloist committed a boring improvisation on a theme from *The Marriage of Figaro*? And not only interrupting that lame performance, but then *meowing* a countermelody over it?

We also see a vulgar streak in several prank tunes, many composed in tandem with his masterpieces. There is, in fact, a meow duet in the Mozart oeuvre. Also, the same year he made the luminous Fantasy no. 1 with Fugue, Mozart wrote a canon of six sober voices repeating "Leck mich im Arsch" (or "Lick Me in the Butt"). Another canon from that period begins with the phrase "good night" in several languages, then a sung "phooey phooey!" and a filthy line about crapping the bed.

Away from the keyboard, Mozart was just as devious with wordplay, as seen in the polyglot prattle of his letters, like this one to his cousin:

> Muck!—muck!—oh, muck! O sweet word!—muck!—
> chuck! That's good too!—muck, chuck!—muck!—
> suck—oh *charmante!*—muck, suck!—that's what I
> like!—muck, chuck and suck!—chuck muck and suck
> muck!

Some think the maestro's mysterious brain was troubled by Tourette's or, at the least, an attention disorder. His own brother-in-law wondered if Mozart "concealed his inner tension behind superficial frivolity" by mixing "the divine ideas of his music and . . . sudden outbursts of vulgar platitudes." But this assumes, perhaps too hastily, that the vulgar didn't participate in his divine ideas.

Even though we now know Mozart's brain was not God's fax machine, many still describe it as some sort of sepulcher for only pristine sounds. But why didn't he need it all—the vulgar and the formal, the right notes and the wrong ones, and even those whistled a half step sharp? A man obsessed with perfect tone might need to stay on nodding terms with aberration. What if Mozart played with bad notes and uncouth lyrics, with foreign language and nonsense, to hoard all the expression he could, just as *Sturnus vulgaris* hoards all possible sound in order to sing?

Much earlier in his life, when he was still a baby-genius playing blindfolded for the aristocracy, Mozart's best trick was an improvisational game not unlike an eighteenth-century rap battle. A court composer or some member of the cognoscenti would play a sparse bass line on the keys, over which Mozart would improvise a melody—sometimes complete with harmony or counterpoint. Then his much older opponent would answer back with a different melody, which Mozart would rework, and back and forth again and again until the challenger eventually crapped out. Pipsqueak Mozart never did, and his royal audiences delighted in these on-the-spot reworkings of their musical rules. That's how Mozart grew up—chasing melodies as they flew by him, hunting for the ways each note might pivot into something new. Since this inventiveness kept the Mozart family employed, one might see Wolfgang's open receptors as a musical survival skill.

Thanks to an upper-level connectivity we've only recently identified, starlings are hard-wired for reception, too. Video modeling has led some scientists to suggest that starling bodies fly at a "critical" state, meaning all their physical receivers—down to the cell, maybe even down to the protein—are attuned to simultaneous and dramatic variations within the group. This connection, seen in a mass of flying starlings—dipping, reeling, curling into itself midair—is beyond biology; it's more like physics. A starling in flight is critical like an avalanche, like the ignition of atoms in a magnet, because each body holds the report of its neighboring bodies—and all those bodies' potential—inside itself. But then again, this is merely a theory. What they do runs far past what we can understand and our evidence is somewhat spotty. Though we've lived with starlings for millennia, we're still fumbling for a language to discuss certain aspects of their lives.

Mozart could have kept his starling's cage in the room with his billiard table, where he often composed. Or it might have stood in his bedchamber, where he stayed awake with his quill and notebook (both man and songbird were prone to singing while the rest of the house slept). No matter the living arrangements, the bird stayed with him for thirty-six of the most vibrant months of Mozart's career. The maestro's fortepiano was constantly being shipped from his music room out to the Mehlgrube for yet another subscription concert. Leopold Mozart complained in a letter that his son's home buzzed at all hours with rabble-rousing factions: students, rehearsal groups, goofy late night jam sessions. Their noise was nonstop and deafening. Mozart reportedly hated being alone, even when he worked. And for those three years, work he did.

That costly apartment on the Domgasse saw sixty-plus compositions finished in less than three years. The piano concerto as we still understand it was built in those rooms. The Haydn quartets premiered there. The "Jupiter" symphony began and *Figaro* ended. And with these heavy hitters came some of the most singable ditties in the repertoire: the wafting waltz-time start to the Piano Concerto no. 21 and the stately intervals of the Romanze in the Serenade no. 13 for strings. Melodies that two centuries of humans have since whistled could have first been volleyed between a genius and his Vogel Staar.

And you can bet your *Arsch* that, if it were in earshot, Mozart's starling junked these immortal melodies. As Mozart hammered them shiny, the bird sent the tunes back upside-down, at half-speed and double-time, and piped one inconsequential middle note for five straight seconds. It's not difficult to imagine Mozart valuing this kind of collaboration, as he spent so much of this period reaching out to various "songbirds." The starling was another musician to pump ideas into Mozart's brain—like Haydn did, or Vienna's top fiddlers, or his high-soprano sister-in-law with her gobsmacking range. Among the divas, the composers, and the virtuosi, that caged bird perched the furthest outside the Classical box, waiting to eat all the sound it was offered and spit back strange bits with starling gusto.

Picture an early morning composing session, the starling's cage near the sixtieth key. Mozart flies into the room, fresh from dressing, with his hairstylist trailing behind him. The *Friseur* still holds the end of the maestro's wig-braid, like the owner of a spastic dog.

The bird stirs as Mozart kicks back the bench and stands over the ebonies. He needs to tease out this theme that's been flitting around in his head for days. He finds the tonic, a sprightly G, and then dances between it and the fourth below. Then he reverses the melody's course and skips it upward, bouncing to the dominant fifth in an arpeggio that smacks the next octave with a Mannheim Rocket exclamation point:

BUM!   bom BUM!   bom bum-bom-ba-ba BAAH!

Mozart can barely keep up with his pen; he's writing with one hand and playing the melody on the keys with the other. As the notes of the exposition zoom onto his staff paper—flapping merrily along as the form intended—a jalopy-fart of notes comes from the cage, countering the pristine run of the keys: BUM—*hweet!* bom

BUM—*chackerchacker!* Bom bum-bom-bizeet?—brrrrp?—LECK
MICH IM ARSCH—BAAUGH!!

Mozart turns to the bird, which moves closer to the front of
the cage and stares. Starlings are more responsive to human eye
contact than most mammalian pets; they know when they're being
watched and aren't afraid to hold a gaze. It's one of the primary
traits—along with a high touch response—that allows deep bonding between starlings and humans, as we love eye contact, too. One
ornithologist called the starling "the poor man's dog" for its ability
to connect and demonstrate loyalty. And sound assists this connection; what better way to bond than in a duet?

Mozart opens the cage and the bird flits to his arm, screeching that same derailment (bom-bum-bom—bizeet?—brrrrp?—
LECK MICH IM ARSCH!) as it hops up his sleeve. The man
sighs, keeps writing, and the bird keeps yukking and sucking and
mucking it up.

And now, two centuries later, not a day goes by without someone on the planet playing the result: the opening movement of
the Serenade no. 13 for strings, often called *Eine kleine Nachtmusik*.
Notice how, after the exposition, the tune dips treacherously into
D minor before moving forward in a new major key. It sounds as if,
for a quick measure, a little devil has whispered something shocking into the melody's ear.

Notice, too, the wicked work of Mozart's *A Musical Joke*, which
was written nearly in tandem with the perfect *Eine kleine*, most
likely on that same keyboard. Though smarter and not as vulgar
as "Leck mich im Arsch," the divertimento is doubly excruciat-
ing, a relentless twenty-three-minute parody of Classical music's
traps. Notes run up and down the scale like Keystone Cops. Developments flop like punch lines you can see coming from miles
away. And in each of the four painful movements is a hilarious
breakdown—a rusty, unrefined disturbance that explodes the *Joke*'s

mundane torture. These breakdowns play out like lines of starling talk: they are the G-sharps the bird whistled back in the shop, elevated to virtuosic silliness.

In the Minuet, the horns repeat a theme at misplaced half steps, like howling dogs. In the Adagio, the violas trill their scales at double time—whistling teakettles gone rogue. The best starling breakdown comes in the last movement, when the same skipping chirps come again and again, moving like a dare toward forever, until the listener begs for it to end. When Mozart finds the finale (thank God), he ends not by perching at the tonic, but by crashing the ensemble together, screeching the movement to a halt. This might be the least Classical ending in the entire Classical period. For the final measure, the instruments play three block chords in three different keys! The result sounds like the string players throwing their fiddles out the window:

There, in that mangled vertical line of wrong notes, you can almost hear the starling on Mozart's shoulder, bobbing his head, maybe even taking a crap, and chattering: *"das war*—bizeet!— LECK MICH—*chackerchacker* bom-ba-ba-BAAH!—*schön!!!"*

•• ▬ • ▬ ••

In 1787, Mozart's luxe apartment finally became too dear, and the family moved to a place on the Hauptstrasse with rent one-tenth as expensive. Even though they were paring down, Mozart took the bird with them. We know this because he made such a fuss over the starling when it died a few months later.

On that day in early June, the new Mozart home welcomed a dozen mourners in elaborate, costumey garb—giant plumes and feather fans, or maybe black masks with beaks. The guests were first treated to a dirge (arranged by Mozart) for chamber ensemble, and then the maestro recited a short elegy he'd written to his Vogel Staar.

In the poem, Mozart imagines the "little fool," unaware that it is dead, looking down at Mozart and whistling fondly. Now up in heaven, the songbird sings for free, as has always been its custom. By the last stanza, the bird has already sung long enough to forget its keeper and collaborator. And now the maestro is left on Earth to rhyme alone (albeit masterfully, Mozart brags).

Who knows why Mozart planned this cuckoo funeral. We have no evidence that he ever mourned this way again. The verse and the dirge and the funeral party could have been a mock solemnity—Mozart rarely passed up the chance for a weird party or a good gag. On the other hand, he could have been somewhat serious, as he was a known animal lover. But why did he publicly mourn a pet starling and not his own father, who died without ceremony in Salzburg just a week before?

The starling funeral, like its purchase three years prior, is one of the many snippets of Mozart's life that still confound us. Nearly all Mozart biographers mention it among their mob of questions, which they whistle out into the void, knowing they'll never hear an answer: Why buy a bird? Why bury it and not your father? Why a red coat? Why the puns? Why so many notes? Why a serenade one day and a butt gag the next? Is it even possible to bond with a creature only by the sound that it makes? We don't know, we don't know, we don't know.

For so much is left unanswered when a man falls from heaven and writes *Don Giovanni*. Or when the wingbeats of countless tiny creatures lift upward and sound like thunder as they block out the sun. When five hundred starlings drop from the sky into shallow ponds without making a sound. When a genius buys a songbird because, despite his noisy life, something is missing.

And even more remains mysterious when the genius takes to bed in his thirty-fifth year. After two weeks, his hands and feet are swollen—again and again, he blacks out. Though the women around him sob, he can't stop telling little jokes; he can't stop singing. Doctors let him for blood, they prod at his flesh, they can only guess as to what's inside him. Then he sends his pet canary from his room and the women around him weep louder. For when he banishes his bird, they know one thing for sure: he's letting go.

Out the window and down the Hauptstrasse, this genius's most famous opera is in performance. At one point he tells his wife he can hear the soprano hit her aria's top note. At that opera's finale, a lonely bird-catcher takes the stage. He's covered in feathers and ready to die. He sings a string of short pips—"Pa! Pa! Pa!"—and turns just in time to see his companion running out from the wings. As she runs, they lock eyes and she nods her little, feathered head, singing—"Pa! Pa! Pa!"—right back to him.

Harriet
(*Geochelone nigra porteri*)
1835

Despite his flat denial, we know that he did collect at least one tortoise.

Paul Chambers

I can't see why she shouldn't live to two hundred!

Steve "Crocodile Hunter" Irwin

WHEN THE HMS *BEAGLE* DROPS her anchor in 1835, get under the biggest, shadiest frond in sight as fast as you can. Dozens of hungry sailors will jump ship, spears in hand, many lancing their first turpin within minutes. Other men will follow the deep highways of tracks up to the higher points of the island, where hill-dwelling turpin grow longer, saltier necks. In a few hours, they'll all trudge back to ship, hefting dozens of your kind in makeshift stretchers of oars and canvas. Three men to every heavy shell.

The earth trembles. A huge man lumbers past with a fifteen-stone turpin on his back, its arms and legs tied into shoulder straps and its shell like a pack. You tuck yourself in, little girl. Be still. Don't hiss. Not that you have too much to worry about. There's not enough meat under your dinner-plate shell to merit the tedious chore of turpin-gutting.

And then, to your right, a set of lighter steps. A pair of clean pants, a slight cough: the "Ship Naturalist." Before he even sees you, he will sense you. He'll clear away the brush and yell to the others that it might be wise to bring back a few tiny, young tortoises that will wander the ship for months or years, eventually growing into weeks of meals for every name on the manifest. He'll pick you up in his small, soft hands without strain. "Tortoise," he'll call you, not "turpin." With your mouth closed, tap your tongue twice and hiss. *How fancy.*

He will shortly thereafter name you "Harry," but don't doubt that some part of him knows you're all woman. Feel his delicate touch as he swiftly flips you and runs his fingers along your soft, salty underbelly, scrutinizing each shingle, each shank. Delight in how he hand-feeds you pink flowers. Back in his cabin, he will sketch you by lamplight—the shadow and flame giving your checkered exoskeleton a red-green glow. He will coax your neck from the shell and tickle it, measure it, memorize it, muttering, "Amazing." Try to whisper back to him—*Charlie.*

It turns out that Lawson, the gentleman jailer of the Galapagos penal colony, was your matchmaker. The rumors are true; lonely Lawson's got a tortoise in every port—girls to whom, in your opinion, he pays an unhealthy attention. You never gave Lawson the time of day, but Charlie does. In his notebook, he scribbles: "Mr. Lawson states he can, on seeing a tortoise, pronounce with certainty from which island it has been brought."

I'll bet he can, you think, looking underneath Charlie's adorable script to a portrait of you in odalisque, your neck tilted just so. But it's nice to know Lawson told Charlie you were a catch. Nothing he could find in Africa or the West Indies, and certainly not in England. Now when he eyes you, your unique shell, a wildness stirs in him.

As the sailors plow through the other tortoises on the *Beagle*— sometimes three adults for every day at sea—rest easy. They'll slice each neck in one blow, gulping the gallons of fresh water that spill from each gullet, but remember Charlie's tacit promise to take you away from all this. Sure, he joins the crew in sipping the bladder of your old neighbor at dinnertime, then comments on her "only very slightly bitter" taste, but he's doing it to keep you safe, to not arouse suspicions. You're not dinner; you're different.

He's getting stronger, you think. The planks of the captain's quarters shake when Charlie bangs his fist on the table. Captain Fitz-Roy thought he'd hired a seminarian-turned-science-man to come along for the crossing and prove the world made in seven days. A few nights with you, however, and Charlie's become a charlatan. The two men fight like dogs but Charlie leaves you out of it. Instead, they talk finches:

"The islands are as old as Genesis," FitzRoy growls.

"No," says Charlie. "These islands are young, and as they multiply, the finches change their beaks to serve it."

"Serve an island, not our God?" And the turpin stew goes flying.

If we can adapt to an ever-changing island, who says we can't adapt for love, you think. Adaptations, after all, are nothing more than labor: fueled by chemistry, successful only when lauded by a mate. What makes one special, what makes one species, what makes the only changes on the earth that matter—it's always something love-born: a horn, a neck, a killer claw.

For we were not born to mate, wallow, and die. We were not born to duplicate the image God threw together long ago, before the earth smoothed or the stars pulled ships through the wet dark. We were born to move—by leap or by creep. To riff and code on a vector. To surprise God as we catch up to the morphing rocks and malleable seas on our own volition.

Listen to me, Charlie. His pupils move to you and deepen. *This is something you already know.* Together, you can map the places in the body, the heart, and the blood where God was wrong.

Two endpoints reconnect and send the vectors in reverse, sub-tracting shells and snouts and thumbs back to a stock image: the same embryo spinning in the nest of a woman, a salamander, a salmon.

Once you finally land in England a year later, it's not exactly featherbeds and mud baths till the wheels fall off. Boxes of corps-es—birds, plants, bugs, old rocks—pass through his study, which he piles into groups to be sent out for analysis. *Hmmm*, you think, chewing wilted watercress. *No tortoises.* You were the only one he thought to keep, the remains of the others heaved overboard with the slop.

But that fall, you'll find yourself in the draftiest room of the British Museum, shivering on a butcher-block table with three other girls about your age. Surprise—you're all from the *Beagle*, four secrets stashed away in the gentlemen's cabins. Even godly Captain FitzRoy had a Galapagos on the sly—Dick, from Española Island, the prettiest of the bunch. On the table, she tucks her head into her shell and weeps, her voice muffled and snuffling.

I've been out in the garden since October. He took a wife the week we docked. A wife!

At least he doesn't have kids yet, says Tom, the big girl from San Salvador, who followed a father of three to the Albany West. *His brats use me for pony rides.*

John Gray, the museum's Keeper of Zoology, jostles each of you in his oily hands, then declares your lot too young to assess scientifically. Your shells won't develop their distinct shapes until full adulthood. "Sorry, Charlie," he says. "Maybe in thirty, forty years," he says. "But these finch specimens—yes. Another matter altogether." Charlie turns away from you and faces the bird box on the opposite laboratory table.

Oh, God, wait for me, Charlie, you beg. *I'll grow faster. I know I can figure something out.* He sends you home to Great Marlborough Street in a hatbox.

On come the heart problems—his and yours—until his sweet notebooks change temperature. Doodles of beaks and feathers in the margins, and at the top of one page—

"Marry" on the left side,	"Not Marry" on the right:
"constant companion"	"less money for books."
"friend in old age	"terrible loss of time."
(better than a dog, anyhow)"	

He'll move you in with his doped-up brother and wed his nervous, pious cousin, devoting his days either to her or to the finches. He takes her in a carriage and brand-new hat to the Zoological Society of London, but hides you in his cheap "B Notebook"— heated scribblings he wouldn't dare be seen with in public. Instead of words like "marry," "companion," he writes you words like "specimen," "transmutation," "common descent."

Desperate, you rifle through his letters. "My Dear Gunther," he writes one reptologist, "I find that I did *not* bring home any tortoises from the Galapagos." Now you roll and reel in the yard.

Soon, wifey will force him to banish you and the other mistresses to the Royal United Services Museum in Whitehall, where London's gales freeze you into a state of perpetual hibernation. Tom dies. Dick defects to warmer climes. Surely somebody will see you're sick and get you the hell out of there—away from her, from him, from that notebook that has changed him so. What are you waiting for, my girl? High-tail it back to the boat; beg them to take you home.

●● ▬ ● ▬ ●●

Wickham, the new captain of the *Beagle*, takes you to Australia instead. You remember him from the trip with Charlie, when he was only first lieutenant, butchering ten turpins an hour just to drain them for lamp oil. Wickham likes the shape of you and takes you in as his.

The captain's quarters are far larger than the naturalist's—a lady should improve her station—but Wickham is disorderly. Upturned inkwells, gnawed turkey bones, loose dickies. You avoid your silhouette, haggard and bulky, in the light from his lantern. Keep calm, honey. Buck up. Gain a few hundred pounds.

You'll endure Wickham's rough touch all the way to the Antipodes. He bobs along the coastline, drawing maps by day and snoring all night. He's tired of you, he says, resting his cufflinks in a buffed turtle shell. "Don't you hiss at me, fatty," he says. "I'm all you got." The next day, he names a new inlet "Port Darwin" just to spite you.

The men on deck curl their lips as they sing and swing their ropes into the air. Fists pull; thumbs rotate and chafe. Above you, gulls beat their wings like pterodactyls. Grinning fish trail the boat, chattering as they surface, breathing the air in deep gulps.

Once you dock, his manservant dumps you on the grounds of a Moreton Bay mental asylum without so much as a thank-you-ma'am. Wickham sashays off to Sydney, marries *his* sweetheart, becomes a God-fearing policeman. Now you watch those same gulls from the boat circle the grounds before they wing it back out to sea.

At the Brisbane Botanic Gardens, your roommate, George, understands.

I say you're better off without him, she wheezes. *Those scientific types are all the same—emotionally incapable of seeing past their own needs. Doesn't even matter if they marry; they're only really ever married to their work. Usually it's because their fathers didn't show them enough affection.*

George had it bad for the whaler who brought her over the Pacific. She made the crossing only to get drugged and dragged to a pub in Queensland, where the bastard made her race blinded wallabies for coins through most of the 1850s.

Damn freak, she says, her voice a lifeless muscle. When George sleeps, you stare at the initials the whaler carved in her shell. Within a year, she's dead.

And every day, all the talk is of Charlie—in the mouths of the visitors, the botanists, the apprentices who douse your shell in laundry water after closing time. His book, his fucking finches, his revolution, his ten kids. And eventually, his last words. Not "my love" or even just "my notebook," or—God be merciful—"my tortoise."

He says, "I am not the least afraid to die."

A tomato fattens in the sun and breaks the vine, rolling into a scorpion's nest. The scorpion grows a second, orange-red stinger to scratch a crude, red circle in the dust.

After the cave salamander wills away his eyes, he feels a gull's discarded feather float across his tail. He spends the rest of his life begging his sight to return.

Every morning, before dressing, Charlie would read in his ship cabin. The buttons of the chair left checkered patterns down the flesh of his back.

So that's it, babe. You're forty years shy of middle age and it's over. If you had the ducts for it, you'd weep a deluge of tortoise tears. But don't exhaust yourself staying up all night crying; nature will do it for you. The Brisbane River swells all through the first weeks of 1893, then surges in February: three floods in thirteen days. Let yourself tumble in that rising water. Dodge the uprooted trees, and stay close to Dick, the ol' girl from the *Beagle*, the only other tortoise left in your gardens. She's traveled as far and as long as you have, but she's got more street smarts. Mines explode. Bridges collapse. *If this keeps up, they'll start eating us again*, she says.

The two of you float to a shed's rooftop and, from that perch, watch the city sink into the rain. Isn't Brisbane tonight the same dark, the same thick, the same wet as the islands that made you? And guess what? Tomorrow's Valentine's Day.

Later that night, Dick smacks you awake. *It's happening!* she says, and nods toward the sea wall. Three gunboats, the *Paluma*, the *Elamang* and the *Mary Evans*, spin on their tethers in the vast current, like toy tugs fighting the pull of a drain.

One ship tears from its mooring and floats sideways toward the botanical gardens, blotting out the moon. The *Mary Evans*. There's a woman strapped to its hull with the teats of a cow and the tail of a fish. Swim to her for awhile, fight that current, mind the debris, push outward and upward, survive, survive, survive. But then again, what's the point? Another ship, another map, another man. Tuck your legs in and sink. You'll barely feel it when your head hits the prow.

Charlie wrote pages about his own "fever dreams," but you never imagined that yours would be cool and windowless. Around you sit strange things in dirty pens: a muskrat with swim fins who lays leathery eggs in the mud. A huge dog that hops and keeps its pups in a furry pocket. A winking cat chewing on the limbs of a tree. A hissing dog with the teeth of a tiger.

And in the center of it all, Master Fleay, who speaks through his nose and shows the wealthy ladies of Queensland the marks that tiger-dog left on his ass when he tried to capture its image in a little black machine. Another naturalist, but this one's a grinner, born a century after Charlie, and the first to give you a lady's name.

"Go back to sleep, ol' girl," he says. "Sleep long as you fancy and leave everything to me. I'll save you. Better yet, I'll make you famous."

"Ladies?" he gestures to the women around you. I've saved the best for last. Isn't she a beyoot? Harriet is her name. Used to belong to Darwin, she did, back in the last century. But now she is mine, all mine."

Snap out of it and into a dry field with a sturdier fence. How long have you been out? Now the sun is relentless; the women around you wear trousers and no hats. Many of them sport square, beetle-black faces with one shiny eye. When the eyes blink, it makes daytime lightning.

A fully grown man in short pants, named Irwin, hops to either side of you, his hair stuck to his ruddy forehead in wet, blond drips. "CRIKEY!" he yells, then "CRIKEY!" again, like the boys from the asylum, stricken with tics. He holds a few poses for the crowd and their flashing eyeballs: hugging your neck, an elbow on your shell to prop up his flushed chin, straddling you with outstretched arms and mouth open wide. His wet touch is warm, like a baker patting out dough. At the edge of the pen, his long-haired wife grits her teeth.

He will lead the crowd in a dirgelike "Happy birthday, dear Harry-ette," then skip a few hundred yards over to the "Crocoseum" for an impromptu reptile freak-out. Watch him bound onto the stage, a baby croc in each hand, shaking them like maracas in the dusty breeze.

The two crocs roll their bobbling eyes toward your pen: *Out of the way, Gran.* Irwin tosses you a few pink flowers to gum, and the grimacing wife cuts a huge cake in half, fourths, eighths, sixteenths, thirty-seconds. She slices through your name in sugar, as well as your age—the cause for all this celebrating. The numbers in icing read 1-7-5.

This world has needs, thought the ancient god Manjushri, when he levitated a tortoise just above the primordial sea. As she hovered there, gorgeous and in love, he shot her in the chest with an arrow of gold. The blood, the shit, the fire she vomited married her to the water, creating dirt, lava, rock—all on top of her. This mass spiraled and grew until the entire world rested there. Not on her shell, but on the flat flesh of her belly. The future—all our endpoints—landed there too, below the gold beam lodged in her heart. Did that arrow stay stuck, pushing up through the bottom of the planet like a pole? Lie on your back and look up, sweet pea. See how it still tickles you as it spins?

Look away from the arrow, and there is Charlie 124 years ago, hand to chest, staggering in the woods around Down House.

Look away, and there is the morning next June that you decide to roll over, switching from backstroke to crawl. *It's heavier today*, you'll think, cringing.

Look away, and there is Irwin in the Batt Reef ten weeks after that, chasing tail on a Monday afternoon.

When someone puts a barb in your heart, the worst thing you can do is pull it out.

War Pigs
(*Columba livia domestica*)
1870   1918   1954   2012

These are the birds we immortalize—on our jackets, in our coops, in our lives—because these are the troopers. You know what I mean? Real soldier pigeons.

Mike Tyson

GAMBETTA

It took less than a week for the Prussians to find the secret wire buried in the Seine and to cut it. Then the Parisians tried rolling iron balls stuffed with notes downriver toward Le Havre, but the balls were uncontrollable. And after the five sheepdogs they'd trained to run messages back from the countryside were never seen again, besieged Paris turned to its pigeons.

Just one look at the birds proved how positively gaudy they were with this beady-eyed desperation to fly back to their lofts at the L'Espérance pigeon club or the Roitelet Society. They'd been beelining home since the Bonapartists, since Genghis Khan, since twenty million years before anything even remotely resembling a Frenchman. So why not stamp an official number under their wings, lift them out of town in one of Paris's notorious hot-air balloons, and then send them flying back to the walled city? Each of those bird tails could be tied to twelve tiny rolls of microfilm, and each film could bear thousands of messages from the outside world. The birds would just do for Paris what they were already so keen to do for themselves.

Their hollow bones could fill to bursting with reservoirs of oxygen, and their gigantic breasts, nearly half their masses, could circulate that oxygen for days on little sleep and barely a morsel. Inside every hen or cock were two compasses, one that knew the sun and one that marked the humming magnetic loops that bend around our earth. Each pigeon could hear the subaudible waves of wind as it banked off distant mountains and smell the subtle changes humans carved in the land from farms to cities. When the birds flew home, they watched spires and rivers for reference.

It wasn't that Paris's pigeons were speedy—they weren't. Nor were they foolproof. The Prussians, always one goddamn step ahead, had trained hawks to hunt them midair. Or they'd capture a bird alive and send it back to Paris tied to fake, disturbing news. Not to mention the hungry *rustres* along the Loire, who unwittingly shot the birds down for their country stews.

In the end, only a sixth of the pigeons brought microfilm back to the trapped. But they were all Paris had, both its public officials and its private citizens, who were all walled into the city for the coldest winter on record. And where the wayward pigeon heart warms itself by rushing home at seven hundred beats per minute, the trapped human heart keeps warm by calling to hearts that beat for it elsewhere:

> *Get the stuff from the armoire, and the glass things, and anything fragile and keep them close to you. / I'm very anxious, but I'm pushing my nerves down as much as I can while you're in there. / Give up the apartment on the Boulevard Bineau. Your wife, children, we all kiss you/ God keep you and a thousand kisses. / Espérons!*

•• ▬ • ▬ ••

CHER AMI

By the second day under mortar fire, the 77th Division—or the "Lost Battalion"—was half its original size, and that half was more than half-starved. They were counting out their remaining bullets and pulling bandages off the dead to apply to the half-dead. For water, they had to crawl into eyeshot of German snipers, who fired at the first sight of khaki. This was about the time when the French, unaware of the 77th's position, began shelling their allies.

The planes had been no help, with their terrible aim. They threw down food and supplies within arm's reach of nobody. One airdrop landed two crates of carrier pigeons—eight parachutes strapped to each box—right into the German camp. But you can't blame the pilots. It was 1918, and man had only been flying for a decade.

Around two in the afternoon, a young lieutenant named Orem ducked through the camp, a pigeon basket strapped to his back. In the box were the outfit's last two birds, and both were hooting and nervous. Major Whittlesey had launched two other carriers the day before—each tied to a missive saying that three hundred men were still trapped, still suffering—but both of those birds had copped a packet.

Orem's hand slipped as he scooped a pigeon from that last box, and when that bird escaped, flew up and away from him, all that was left for the 77th was one Blue Check hen, US Army #43678. The last pigeon of the Lost Battalion. The message she'd carry was ready for her, scribbled by Whittlesey on a tiny scrap:

WE ARE ALONG THE ROAD PARALELL 276.4.
OUR AR ILLERY IS DROPPING A BARRAGE DI-
RECTLY ON US. FOR HEAVENS SAKE STOP IT.

They watched her take off, the message rolled into a crucial tube at her leg. She circled the whorls of artillery smoke and then settled herself on a tree just downhill from them. When both major and lieutenant threw sticks at her, she jumped to a higher branch and preened compulsively, so they threw rocks. Then the young Orem, still mortified over butterfingering that first pidge, shimmied up the tree and shook her from it.

She got high enough that most of the Lost Battalion could see her: the able-bodied buck privates piling the dead into a makeshift wall; the three remaining medics, crazed with duty; the wounded left useless on their backs in the ravine. Anyone not hunkered into his funkhole had to watch her lifting up and away.

And what a vertigo she must have created for the trapped and the crippled who saw her escaping. This stocky dove, this fist with wings, tamping down the contaminated air in her ascent, pushing away all that was lost and clearing a space for all that is home. A pigeon in the air, lifting out of the trench, is a gray flag of possibility, a final opportunity for the doomed to pull their heads up. A pigeon in war is a chance to keep imagining.

Then a shell exploded underneath her, killing five men and sending the shocked bird to the ground. And that descent is the last recorded remembrance of the 77th's last pigeon by any lasting member of the Lost Battalion. Perhaps they all turned away because they couldn't stand to watch further, and this is why no 77th saw the moment when she relaunched her body—one eye just *gone* and one leg hanging by a tendon, tin tube still affixed. Nobody saw her wobble in the air toward Mobile Message Unit #9, twenty-five miles southwest, picking up speed as she flew. And since nobody saw her, no 77th doughboy could possibly imagine what was going to happen next.

• • ▬ • ▬ • •

LEAPING LENA

We don't know who owned her, or which town in West Germany she came from. We don't know her original name, or even if she had one. Chances are, she was just another serially numbered homer on that summer day she ignored the race route back from Munich, hung a right at Schwanberg, and flapped herself over the Iron Curtain.

Perhaps, in the air, she dodged a few of those polyethylene *luftballons* stamped SVOBODA in garish red all-caps. The Free Europe Committee had launched the balloons from wheat fields at the border for most of the 1950s. When each eventually popped, it rained leaflets on communist Prague, Pilsen, Ostrava, or some red village in between:

THIS LEAFLET
WAS DROPPED
FROM A BALLOON

IT IS A MESSAGE
FOR YOU . . . FROM THE
CRUSADE FOR FREEDOM

TAKE IT HOME
. . . PLEASE READ THE
OTHER SIDE

But a lost West German racing pigeon is better than a red balloon, because an anonymous Czech can't send the popped red balloon *back*. A pigeon, on the other hand, can fly back over the wall with a Czech citizen's secret message—back to her coop and, soon after, to the offices of Radio Free Europe. She could then bear that Czech message to Adenauer and Ike, for Mr. and Mrs. America, from border to border, coast to coast, and all the ships at sea:

We plead with you not to slow down in the fight against Communism because communism must be destroyed [. . .] We listen to your broadcasts [. . .] We would like

you to tell us how we can combat "Bolshevism" and the
tyrannical dictatorship existing here [...]
—UNBOWED PILSEN

They booked that pigeon a ticket to Idlewild and re-christened
her, for the awaiting American public, a name with all the alveolar
pulchritude of Lois Lane, Lorelei Lee, and Lolita. When Leaping
Lena landed in New York, the prettiest stewardess they could find
stood by her for the *Times* photograph. The headlines read COOS
AND KUDOS TO 'ANTI-RED' PIGEON and IRON CURTAIN
BIRD HERE ON CRUSADE and WRONG WAY PIGEON
WHO CRASHED RED CURTAIN GETS BIG OVATION. A
thousand captive American birds took to the sky in her honor.

They made her a citizen and found her a hero cock to nest with.
While a band played "The Iron Curtain Does Not Reach the Sky,"
she posed for an ad to shill for US bonds. These were minted "Truth
Dollars," that, the CIA assured, would help America "fight the big
lie." But there is also the chance that the "big lie" was Lena herself.

The names of her German handlers were never recorded.
Her hometown, when it appears in print, is spelled three different
ways. She was flying to Munich, Rhineland, or Bavaria, depending
on which American paper told her story. And just as we can't trace
her origins, no one knows what happened at the end of her US
tour, since the Army coop that kept all hero pigeons was disman-
tled soon afterward.

But why not invent a pigeon to be a CIA pinup girl? What better bird to fight a cold war, really, than a bird of ideas? For many
of us, an idea is a kind of home—to fly to, to roost in. And an
idea built inside a comforting framework—a feathered friend, for
example—can fly much further than a fact can. Lena gave America ideas about the desires that might lie in the silent homes over a
foreign wall (that wall an idea in and of itself). She gave Americans

the idea that they stood on a home turf worth flying to, worth scaling walls for, and this told them the American-made idea of home was worth their fierce, nearly blind protection. And because of all this, they idealized that unreal German homer with the very real fact of their homegrown American cash.

•• ▬ • ▬ ••

THE BAB AMR BIRD

The two hands that hold the camera shake in the February wind. "See what you've done, Bashar? You've sent us back to the Dark Ages."

They film another pair of hands—the left one scribbling Arabic in blue ink on a paper scrap, and the right one holding the scrap steady to keep it from flying away:

> From the activists in Old Homs to those in Bab Amr,
> please tell us what you need in terms of supplies and
> food. God willing, we will get them to you.

The camera swings to two more hands holding a Dexford walkie-talkie: "These only work up to one hundred meters. When one of us is out of range, we have to use the birds."

Then the camera zooms in on a third pair of hands pulling a gray-capped pigeon from a cloth bag. The bird sits quietly in the grip of its handler, like a hot rock held to keep warm.

All told, there are eight hands on the gusty roof, passing their work (and that bird) back and forth. Two hands roll the paper tighter than an Alhamraa and knot a thread around it. Two hands pass the pigeon, flipped belly-up, to two more hands, which hold the rolled message against the bird's inner leg, then use the brown thread to make five crude loops: "We wrap it around bird's claw and then we leave the rest up to God."

All hands say blessings over the bird, which is now held in the same hands that wrote the message. It sits up in the cup of two palms as it would in a cozy nest, and waits for the hands to first lower its bird body, then toss it upward in a balletic alley-oop:

"Godspeed, bird!"

"We hope to God that this bird makes from Homs to Bab Amr!"

"God is great!"

"May he arrive in safety!"

There is the sound of gunfire on the streets of Old Homs, of chanting, and of hands placed in a mouth to whistle, as the pigeon circles the roof loft once, then cuts a sharp right.

When the video shows the bird turn, the pigeon looks as if it might keep flying forever, not stopping at Bab Amr, a few miles away, where other hands wait to catch it and tie their own captivity to its right leg. One can't help but picture the bird flying further, to older homes. To thirty-five centuries of them, carrying thirty-five centuries of news.

The Bab Amr bird flies over the shores of ancient Egypt, with a message from the arriving fleet. It flies over King Sargon of Akkad after his last human messenger has perished on the Aleppo road. It flies with news of Olympic triumphs and the results of chariot races on which kingdoms were wagered. It flies with false news from Saladin's army as Richard the Lionheart's men crouch by the city gate.

And then the Bab Amr bird flies back to Homs, just like the first bird ever bought at market, over a millennium ago, that returned itself to its original coop. Back, as the dove sent from the Ark into the deluge to check for safety, back from the balcony where Semiramis of ancient Assyria waited, on the eve of her overthrow, for a prophecy. That prophecy came in the form of a bird and it gave her the wings to disappear.

The second video begins some time later, with a bird in the sky. The hand that holds the camera follows the bird's wide, high circles and captures the sounds of wind, some distant chanting and some not-so-distant explosions, which now shake the roof loft several times per minute. No hands in the frame this time, but near the camera are the same four voices on the same roof. They shout so loud, and with such vigor, it's as if the bird has returned to them not from a mile-long journey, but a much greater distance.

"Look, guys!"

"Here he is! The Bab Amr bird!"

"God is great!"

"God is great!"

"God is great!"

"God is great!"

"God is greater than you, Bashar. You've been sending rockets but we've sent this bird!"

Jumbo II
(*Elephas maximus*)
1901

It will kill men, and something like panic will follow.
Thomas Edison

FROM THE JULY 28, 1796 edition of the *Philadelphia Aurora*, some of which is true:

There has just arrived from New York, in this city, on his way to Charleston, an elephant. He possesses the Adroitness of the Beaver, the Intelligence of the Ape, and the Fidelity of the Dog. He is the largest among Quadrupeds; the earth trembles under his feet: he has the power of tearing up the largest trees, and yet is tractable to those who use him well.

This Elephant now offered for public Exhibition is about three years, near six feet high. He is of the largest species, growing to the height of sixteen feet. He was purchased in New York for Ten Thousand Dollars.

There is no name on record for the elephant.

1805
The second known elephant on the North American continent was purchased in a New York stockyard by a man named Hack.

He called the animal "Bet" after his own daughter Betsy and, after realizing the elephant was no good for farm labor, he walked her from town to town, selling tickets. The ads Hack ran in local papers warned readers, *this is the only one in the United States, and perhaps the last to visit this place.*

He traveled at night with his elephant, in the darkness that was early America, to avoid giving a free show. Elephant vision is notably keen in dim light.

A farmer in Alfred, Maine, became incensed with either the elephant or Hack, depending on which report you believe. He fatally shot Bet as she headed down the road to the next town.

1809

English chemist Humphry Davy spent the first decade of the nineteenth century developing electric light. He placed two carbon rods close together and pushed apart their ends with an electromagnet. When battery-powered current was set to the rods, it leaped in an arc from one filament to the other, and the arc lamp discharged a harsh, intense light that was perfect for illuminating roads, streets, and promenades.

1826

Hack Bailey acquired two more elephants: a male, Columbus, and a female, which he named Bet yet again. By now, Hack was a little more creative in his showmanship. He taught Bet II to uncork bottles of stout and bring them to her lips. He taught her to dip her head like a genteel lady. He spread a rumor that her hide was bulletproof, which led a gang of boys in Rhode Island to shoot her with six muskets at once.

Columbus dropped dead for unknown reasons after a show in Baltimore. Hack replaced him with a fourth elephant, gave him the same name, and proceeded like nothing had happened. Columbus II lived for twenty more years, until he fell through a rickety bridge.

1849

Newspaper cartoonists imagined the country, which now stretched all the way to the Pacific, as a giant and dark elephant. In their hand-drawn maps, the curve of Maine is its trunk and California its tail. Settlers who dragged themselves across the Overland Trails were said to have, in their journeys, "seen the elephant"—both the wonders and the hardships of this gigantic place, the kindnesses and the acts of obscene violence.

1859

As a boy, Thomas Edison pestered linemen around the railroad station where he sold papers and candy. He wanted to know how electricity moved messages over wires. A Scotsman from the Montreal Telegraph Company told young Edison to imagine the wire as a dachshund that stretched from his homeland to the south of England; one could pull his tail in Edinburgh to hear him bark in London.

I could understand that, Edison remembered, *but I never could get it through me what went through the dog or over the wire.*

1862

The king of Siam sent a sword and a pair of royal photographs to the White House, along with a promise to soon send two adult elephants—a gesture of friendship. President Lincoln graciously refused the pair out of worry for the animals, which he was not sure the nation could care for during wartime.

1865

The first elephant to be tried for a crime in America was an "Asiatic" named Old Hannibal. His notable history of violence usually ran concurrent with his periods of musth: Two men at a dock in New Orleans. An unbalanced man in Ohio.

Old Hannibal fell in love with an elephant cow in Pittsburgh, which the circus immediately promoted: *Behold the Pachyderm Romeo and Juliet!* After she was sold, he stopped eating, went on a whiskey bender and killed another keeper. The trial judge acquitted Old Hannibal, saying the keeper must have mistreated him. And besides, what can you expect of a fellow whose heart has just been broken?

His obituary appeared in the *New York Times* two years later, the very same week as the president's:

> *Hannibal was supposed to be about sixty years of age. He had caused the death of two keepers, and the offence cost him his tusks, which were sawn off nearly to his mouth. On one or two occasions he had taken a fancy to roam through the country unattended. He was of grave and dignified demeanor, and seldom indulged in those playful demonstrations common with the smaller and less distinguished specimens of his species. His owners gave orders that he should be interred without robbing him of any of his natural ornaments.*

1878

In October, the Edison Electric Light Company incorporated with over a quarter million dollars of backing. For his first task, Edison applied his notoriously dogged attention to making a cheap incandescent bulb that could light a home with a softer-strength current, one more appropriate for indoors than that of an arc light. His lab in Menlo Park, New Jersey, housed five dozen employees: engineers, chemists, even glassblowers. He liked to joke with the press about the materials he kept on hand—everything *from an elephant's hide to the eyeballs of a United States senator.*

One year later, a headline in the *New York Herald*: *EDISON'S EU-REKA—THE ELECTRIC LIGHT AT LAST.*

1880

The second elephant born in America (and the first to survive infancy) came into the world under the Bailey and Company big top in Philadelphia. Her mother was a dancing elephant named Babe. P. T. Barnum was so covetous of Babe's baby—since it seemed no customer could resist her—that he offered to merge Bailey's circus with his own.

She grew, of course, and soon became just another one of Barnum and Bailey's three dozen adult elephants. The nation turned their attention away from the "baby" until twenty years later, when she threw a lion across Coney Island's Luna Park and into a crowd. Five years after that, she was branded unredeemable. The circus used a block and tackle to choke her to death before a "jury" of twenty-one elephants. Babe was one of them.

Babe died seven years after her daughter, during the circus's traveling tour of the Antipodes—a burial at sea.

1881

One night under the arc lights in Buffalo, New York, a dentist named Alfred P. Southwick watched a drunken dockworker reach down and touch a live wire. When he saw the man fall, Southwick noticed the quickness of the death, its calm and quiet close. The dentist quickly made a deal with the local dogcatcher to perform electrical experiments on the strays of Buffalo.

1882

Two months after Charles Guiteau was tried for the murder of President Garfield, the most famous elephant in history landed at New York City's Castle Garden pier. A team of sixteen horses, five hundred men, and two of P. T. Barnum's pachyderms (Gyp and Chief) pushed the "mastadonic" African elephant's box up Broadway. The beast sold out matinees and evening shows at Madison Square Garden all spring. Over a quarter of the US population saw him—at the Garden or on tour—over three years.

The elephant arrived from England already named and with a repu-tation as the largest, gentlest living thing on the planet. Though no one can be certain where his name originated, by the time the Coward Charles Guiteau was hanged that fall, any large entity in New York was renamed after the animal: Jumbo frankfurters, Jumbo cigars, Jumbo steam whistles, Jumbo lawmakers mucking up the progress in Congress.

Even Edison got into the game. He was a mile away from Madi-son Square, digging under Pearl Street to wire the first American neighborhood with direct current. Six two-hundred-horsepower generators, each with its own steam engine, buzzed noisily beside the eighty-five buildings they powered. Edison had christened the cacophonous generators "Jumbo dynamos."

1883

From an editorial in *Scientific American* titled "Killing Cattle by Electricity":

Death by "judicial lightning" after such a fashion may be adopted in place of the hideous violence of the long drop. Certainly as a project for killing worn-out quadrupeds it appears as effective as it is kindly.

And again, in the same journal, two years later—the editorial "Electricity for Executing Criminals":

> *How simple a process it would be to connect the place of execution in the Tombs with the system of electrical street illumination, so that electricity could be made the executioner of murderers! Death would be instantaneous and perfectly painless while at the same time the awfulness of the penalty thus inflicted would be profoundly impressive.*

1884

For the 1884 season of the Great Forepaugh Show, Adam Forepaugh took his elephant Tiny (once named Othello), and painted him with whitewash. He billed him first as Tiger Killer the White Elephant and then changed it, once more, to Light of Asia. The papers suggested fraud, as did P. T. Barnum, though Barnum was shilling an elephant with vitiligo as "white as God makes 'em." Forepaugh released a heavy-hearted statement that Light of Asia caught a cold and died. He'd really just rinsed the elephant, renamed him John L. Sullivan, and taught him to box. The elephant didn't actually die until forty-eight years later, of heart failure. By then he was called Old John.

1885

When an elephant went rogue and could not be contained, American circus folk said the beast had "gone ugly." After killing his keeper in Nashua, New Hampshire, Ugly Albert was led to a ravine on the outskirts of Keene. There, a local Light Guard fired upon him at fifteen paces. A dead elephant was more mass than any local team could drag away, so, as was the fashion, they cut Ugly Albert into manageable chunks. Twenty yards of entrails. Bones that outweighed an American quarter horse. A forty-pound heart. An acre of blood. A hide for the Smithsonian.

On September 15 of that same year, in a Canadian town about one hundred miles from Niagara Falls, the Great Jumbo's faithful handler, Scotty, walked him down a railway yard to his luxury box-car. An incoming train trapped Jumbo on the tracks and couldn't brake fast enough. The impact smashed Jumbo's tusks into his brain and bucked the locomotive over the elephant's body. He died with the engine still on top of him.

The nation mourned. Barnum sued the railroad and arranged two separate tours: one of the elephant's reassembled bones and one of his stuffed hide—*a DOUBLE JUMBO!*

1886

On the first day of spring, George Westinghouse's chief scientist threw the switch on a street of commercial and municipal buildings in Great Barrington, Massachusetts—the first downtown powered by alternating current. The energy that lit Great Barrington came not from a cacophonous power station a block away, but from a generator parked in an abandoned lumber mill a mile from town. In order for the current to travel that far, "The Great Barrington Electrification" needed a strength of 500 volts, nearly five times that of Edison's direct current at Pearl Street.

An ocean away, in the war with Abyssinia, teams of forty elephants pulled British cannons across the North African desert. When the war ended, many were sent back to England or America to work in the circus trade.

1887

Though direct current powered towns from Chicago to Boston to New Orleans, Thomas Edison still felt the pressure of Westinghouse's progress with alternating current. So the Wizard of Menlo Park—light-bringer to America—printed an alarmist, all-red pamphlet titled "*A WARNING FROM THE EDISON ELECTRIC LIGHT COMPANY.*" It was perhaps the first published work to feature the term "death-current."

Alfred P. Southwick, the Buffalo dentist, never forgot that scene of the dead drunkard and the live wire. That fall, he wrote Edison for the inventor's opinion on electricity as a capital punishment. Edison sent a reply to Southwick that December, which the dentist then excerpted for a report in the *Journal of the American Medical Association*:

> The most suitable apparatus for the purpose is that class of dynamo-electric machinery which employs intermittent currents. The most effective of these are known as "alternating machines" manufactured principally in this country by George Westinghouse. The passage of the current from these machines through the human body, even by the slightest contacts, produces instantaneous death.

That same month, a fire in Barnum and Bailey's winter quarters killed dozens of animals, including Alice, the supposed widow of Jumbo. The thirty elephants strong enough to pull loose from their chains and escape the building caught fire along the way. Parts of their burned hides fell into the straw as they ran.

1888

Notes from H. P. Brown's animal experiments at the Edison laboratory, July 10:

Dog No. 1. Old black and tan bitch; low vitality; weight not taken. Resistance from right front leg to left hind leg, 7,500 ohms. Connection made through wet roll of cotton waste, held in place by wrappings of bare copper wire; continuous current used. Electromotive force at time of closing circuit 800 volts; time of contact through dog 2 seconds.

Dog No. 2. Large half-bred St. Bernard puppy; strong and in good condition. Resistance 8,500 ohms. Connections made as above. Continuous current. Electromotive force 200 volts. Time of contact through dog 2 seconds.

Dog No. 3. Fox terrier bitch, young and of good vitality. Resistance 6,000 ohms. Connections kept thoroughly wet. Electromotive force 400 volts.
   600 volts.
   800 volts.
   1,000 volts.

Dog No. 4. Half-bred shepherd dog; strong and in good condition. Connections same as above. Resistance 6,000 ohms; continuous current, Electromotive force 1,000 volts.
   1,100 volts. Respiration fell to 72 and dog unhurt. Dog yelped when circuit was closed, but wagged his tail as Dr. Peterson counted respiration.
   1,200 volts. Dog yelped as circuit was closed, but still unhurt.
   1,300 volts. Dog yelped.
   1,400 volts. Dog yelped slightly. Respiration 72 (irregular).
   1,420 volts. The utmost capacity of dynamo at present speed.

That fall, after the passage of the New York State Electrical Execution Act—which replaced hanging with death by "judicial lightning"—the state's Medico-Legal Society was tasked to submit a report of best practices. They ordered more tests, this time on animals closer to the weight of a condemned human. The Edison laboratory obliged by electrocuting two calves at 124 and 154 pounds, respectively. Then they tried 2,000 volts on a horse. Then they wondered about larger specimens.

1889
Dynamort. Ampermort. Virmort. Electromort. Electrostrike. Electrocide. Electricide. Electrothanasia. Electrosiesta. Electrolethe. Electrophon. Electropoena. Electro-cremation. Super-electrification. Galvanation. Gerrycide. Joltacuss. Voltacuss. Blitzentod. Razzle-dazzle. Thanelectricized. Browned. Westinghoused.

July 11, in the *New York Times*: *We pray to be saved from such a monstrosity as "electrocution," which pretentious ignoramuses seem to be trying to put into use.*

A twenty-five-year-old circus elephant, one of (at least) two in America named Chief at the time, was reported to have killed so many handlers that no employee of the John Robinson Circus dared go near him. The *British Veterinary Journal* said the circus was in talks to donate the elephant to Edison laboratory, but in the end had a change of heart. They gave "Old Chief" to the Cincinnati Zoo, which shot him by the end of the decade. Two days after, Cincinnati's Palace Restaurant added "elephant loin" to its dinner menu.

Chief II also had a brief flirtation with Edison. In *Scientific American*: *Many who saw or heard of the experiments made with alternating electrical light currents at the Edison laboratory, to find a substitute for hanging, will regret that the big elephant Chief, of Forepaugh's circus, sentenced to death for his viciousness, could not have been experimented with, as was promised.*

Would the 3,000 volts current, which we are told, will surely kill a man—they have been killed with far less than this—be enough to dull the consciousness of an elephant and then kill? It seems the circus people could not wait for the elaborate preparations necessary. They tied a noose around Chief's neck, and giving an end each to two other elephants, started them tugging in opposite directions till the big elephant was dead.

1890

On the second morning of the year, a fire torched Edison's Pearl Street power station. By the time the Metropolitan Fire Department managed to subdue it, only one jumbo remained.

Two hundred sixteen days later, William Kemmler, "The Buffalo Murderer," was led into a mess room at the Auburn Prison. There, electricians had installed a heavy oak chair bolted to the floor, powered by a Westinghouse dynamo. Sixteen months prior, Kemmler had throttled the married woman with whom he'd been living under an assumed name, then walked out of his tenement house, muttering, *I'll take the rope for it.*

The warden cut away Kemmler's new shirt and sack coat at the spine. He placed a rubber skullcap on Kemmler's shaved head. The cap was stuffed with a wet sponge called an "elephant ear."

> WARDEN: *I have warned him that he has got to die and if he has anything to say he will say it.*
> KEMMLER: *I am bad enough. It is cruel to make me out worse.*
> PRISON DOCTOR: *May God bless you, Kemmler.*
> [cue 1,300 volts of electric current, released for seventeen seconds.]
> PRISON DOCTOR: *He is dead.*
> DENTIST ALFRED P. SOUTHWICK: *We live in a higher civilization from this day.*

A WITNESS: *See—he still breathes!*
ANOTHER WITNESS: *Great God, he is alive!*

An elephant in the Wallace Brothers' Circus threw his trainer across the ring and then chased away the small-town police force that tried to restrain him. He was last seen running into the California desert, never to be heard from again.

1891

Three New York murderers, all electrocuted July 7:
    James Slocum (murder of wife)
    Harris Smiler (of mistress)
    Shubuya Jugiro (of shipmate)
    Joseph Wood (of drinking buddy)

And in December, Martin Loppy (of wife, with scissors). He required four jolts.

1892

February 8, Charles McElvaine (of grocery store clerk). Killed in a new style of chair, borne from Edison's suggestion after the Kemmler disaster, in which the condemned man's hands are submerged in shallow bowls filled with saline. Results were less than ideal.

1893

January 6, Zip the elephant (a four-foot chain of iron was found in her stomach, which the elephant must have swallowed when no one was looking)

May 7, Carlyle Harris (of wife, with sleeping pills, her death originally misdiagnosed as stroke)

July 27, William Taylor (of fellow inmate). His twitching leg pulled the electrode from the chair at the first jolt. His third jolt fried the prison generator. He died on a cot as the electricians tried to re-wire the chair to the city of Auburn's DC power supply.

The Niagara Commission accepted George Westinghouse's bid to build three double-phase generators for the city of Buffalo that would take their power from Niagara Falls, thirty miles away. Edison's General Electric was among the companies that lost the bid to Westinghouse, along with the bid to power Chicago's World's Columbian Exposition, the first all-electric fair featuring a brilliant "White City" of light.

NIKOLA TESLA: *Niagara Power will make Buffalo the greatest city in the world!*

During the last month of the Chicago World's Columbian Ex-position, an elephant named Dolly went on a rampage, plowing through the Midway at the fair's busiest hour. Elsewhere on the Midway, a dwarf elephant got into a vat of beer, drank to excess, and died before the famous electric-powered closing ceremonies.

1894
Tip the elephant (fed a tray of poisoned oats)

1895
July 1, Robert Buchanan (of wife, with poison)

1896
February 11, Bartholomew Shea (of election reform activist)

At midnight on November 16, the mayor of Buffalo threw a switch at the Niagara station and brought AC power to his town. Nikola Tesla, mastermind behind the "polyphase" system which allows super-charged currents to travel great distances, gave a speech at the Falls:

Niagara has something in accord with our present thoughts and tendencies. It signifies the subjugation of natural forces to the service of man, the discontinuance of barbarous methods, the relieving of millions from want and suffering.

Gyp the elephant killed at least seven men within a quarter-century:

Harry Cooley (smashed in Forepaugh's winter quarters)
George West (crushed on tour with Robinson's Circus)
"Jimmy the Bum" (flattened in Louisiana)
Robert White (thrown across the room with enough force to disembowel him)
William Devoe (while with O'Brien's show in Poughkeepsie)
Patsy Hulligan (died of infection after Gyp tore off his arm)
Frank Scott (a lion tamer)

Gyp's trainer returned from vacation after the beast had dispatched the lion tamer, and Gyp reached out her trunk to embrace her man. The papers clamored to send her to Edison by the end of the year. Three weeks later, the *Times* reported the trainer had made a convincing appeal to spare her, and that Gyp *may be sent to Cuba to trample down the ranks of Spaniards.*

1897

August 3, in the US Patent Office:

#587,649. ELECTROCUTION CHAIR.

To All Whom It May Concern—
The invention relates particularly to an electrocution-chair, which is so arranged that the contraction or expansion of various muscles will be registered while the current is passing through the body.

Such records would possess a certain scientific interest and would give an opportunity of accurate observations and deductions of the action of the electric current at high voltages on the human system. Such information, it will be seen, of course could not be obtained in any other way.

1897

The Pan-American Exposition Company originally planned to stage their World's Fair—a celebration of American progress—on an island in the Niagara River, a few miles upstream from the Falls. They later settled on Buffalo instead, as it was one of the ten largest cities in the union, with its busy harbor, twenty-six railroads, and twelve steamship lines.

October 19, Syd the elephant (burned alive until the Robinson and Franklin Brothers' Circus changed their minds, then salved with petroleum jelly and sent back to work)

1898

Congress pledged a half million dollars to support the Pan-American Expo, but halted its production until the conclusion of the Spanish-American War. President McKinley offered his personal support, pledging to do anything he could to help Buffalo. In return, the Pan-American Exposition Company promised their fair would showcase the most impressive American accomplishments of the past hundred years and would be remembered as "the electrical marvel of the opening century."

That spring, Barnum's circus set out for a European tour on the SS *Minneapolis* with eighteen elephants in tow. The circus executed a quarter of them before returning:

Don Pedro (choked by block and tackle in Liverpool)
Nick (strangled in Stoke-on-Trent)

Fritz (tied to a tree and garroted after escaping in Tours)
Mandarin (hanged over the water as the boat docked in New
York. Mandarin's trainer wept)

August 1, Martin Thorn (of William Guldensuppe)

1899
March 20, Martha M. Place (of stepdaughter). Sing Sing's warden telegrammed Governor Theodore Roosevelt to assure him the
world's first Westinghoused female *met her fate with fortitude*.

1900
Four men fell to their deaths while constructing the elaborate geog-
raphy of the Pan-American Exposition, with its canal, its gargantuan curved pergolas, its "Triumphal Bridge" that two carriage
teams could ride across.

Among the buildings were a paean to the US government mod-
eled after a Spanish cathedral, a fireproof art-house, and a
rainbow-colored Midway of pillars, columns, and domes that
would house exhibitors from around the world. The Expo's
Temple of Music seated 2,200, and was installed with one of
the largest organs ever built. A menagerie of animals from six
continents—both trained and wild beasts—would be housed in a
gigantic arena.

And in the center of the plan, supported by an elephantine fountain, a four-hundred-foot Electrical Tower covered in eleven thousand Edison bulbs.

The nineteenth century grew deadlier with each passing year.
In March, the *New York Herald* reported at least a dozen elephant
trainers had been killed by their animals since the previous spring.

No paper of record appears to have kept tally of the deaths of elephants at the turn of the century:

Tom the elephant, killed in Central Park (poisoned bran)

Dick the Dancing Elephant, in Madison Square, after refusing to budge (strangled)

Nero the elephant, hunted down in Racine (pitchforks)

Sport the elephant, accidentally hit by a train and in need of euthanasia (the hanging, from a derrick, overseen by a newcomer to the American circus: Englishman Frank "The Animal King" Bostock)

1901

In the months leading up to the Pan-American Expo, 1,045 train cars arrived in Buffalo bearing supplies to appoint the fair. According to a March 17 Associated Press story:

Two hundred animals consigned to a menagerie and destined ultimately to reach the Pan-American Exposition have reached Baltimore. They came on two steamers and are valued altogether at $100,000. They include two Indian elephants, two African zebras, five Abyssinian hyenas, two East India jaguars, five East Indian leopards, three royal Bengal tigers, six Polar bears, two Himalaya mountain sloth bears, two Indian cassowaries, two African emus, Indian yak, six African ostriches, three male African lions, three African lionesses, two Nubian lions and lionesses, one African giraffe, three South American panthers, one case of East Indian snakes, pythons, anacondas, boa constrictors, etc.; 100 birds and monkeys of various kinds and sizes from Africa, India, Gibraltar and Ceylon.

April 21, in the *Buffalo Evening News*:

"Big Lil," an immense elephant, five sacred donkeys, and 12 sacred cattle, all part of Bostock's wild animal show, arrived in Buffalo this morning.

The management of this show is looking about for 100 mules whose owners have no scruples as to what becomes of their animals.

April 25, in Peru, Indiana: Big Charley the elephant drowned a trainer—the fourth man he'd killed. He led a mob on a chase through the streets of Peru and out to a field. There, the mob threw him cyanide apples until he fell over. The town treasured his remains for a dozen years, until a flood washed away all but his tusks.

On May 1, Thomas Edison sent a film crew to Buffalo to record the Pan-American Expo's opening ceremonies and any other sights that might catch a quarter at his Kinetoscope parlors across the nation. Edison Studios' *Pan-American Exposition by Night* is a breathtaking one-minute panorama—first of the sunlight dimming around the domed Temple of Music, and then heading east to the Electric Tower as the sky goes dark. A searchlight sends a massive beam from the "lantern" at the top of the four-hundred-foot tower, and each building appears in a bulb-lit outline. In the stark black-and-white contrasts of early film stock, the Expo skyline seems an X-ray of itself.

For the Pan-American Exhibition's Dedication Day on May 20, Vice President Roosevelt read aloud a telegram from President McKinley, who was scheduled to attend the festivities but delayed by his wife's illness. *I earnestly hope that this great exhibition may prove a blessing to every country of this hemisphere*, said the president through the wire. His visit to Buffalo, the papers noted, would have to wait until September.

Frank "The Animal King" Bostock arranged for his star elephant Big Lil to carry a caged lion on her back for the Midway Day Parade on July 24. Big Lil' was yet another cow rumored to have been a paramour of the infamous Jumbo, now fifteen years gone. Bostock's new elephant, Jumbo II, was not in Buffalo yet, but his shtick was already in place: an Abyssinian War hero, medaled by the recently deceased Queen Victoria. On his way to Buffalo, Jumbo II was reportedly sedated with coconut liqueur and, while intoxicated, he killed a horse on the train ramp.

July 26, in the *Buffalo Evening News*:

> *Twenty-nine heavy truck horses drew the wagon on which Jumbo II was carried. Curious crowds lined the streets from the depot at Carroll and Chicago Streets to the grounds. The elephant was penned up in an immense plank box and only his ears protruded. Nevertheless from the size of the box and from the evident way in which it cramped the beast it was easy for even the casual observer to note that he is a worthy successor to the name Jumbo.*

August 10, in the *News* again:

> *The President of the United States will be in Buffalo to visit the Pan-American Exposition on the 4th, 5th, 6th and 7th days of September. Such was the arrangement made with him in Canton yesterday by a committee representing the city and the Exposition.*

During this hottest month of the year, the Pan-American saw as many as forty thousand visitors per day. And amid the bustling crowds, a rumor—most likely started by Frank Bostock—that Big Lil the elephant and Jumbo II were falling in love.

August 29, in the *American Journal of Education*:

> *The most colossal and ponderous pachyderm ever in captivity is now on exhibition at the Bostock's animal arena at the Pan American Exposition, and is known as Jumbo II.*
>
> *At the outbreak of the Abyssinian War Jumbo II, who was then called Rostum Single, was deported along with nineteen*

others. Although wounded severely, he stuck to his position whilst shot and shell flew in all directions, trumpeting shrilly and keeping the herd together, which otherwise would have stampeded.

September 4, in the *Atlantic Monthly*:

The Electric Tower is a great center of brilliancy. There are perhaps not a half million electric bulbs, but there are hundreds and thousands of them and you are willing to believe that there may be millions. Out of the city of beauty rises a massive pillar, like an overlooking flower in a gorgeous garden, a centerpiece in a cluster of gems, a venerable fabric of jeweled lace. There it stands, glowing with the lights of many thousand bulbs flashing its image in the basin at its feet, showing its gleaming dome to the people in neighboring cities.

The September 6 itinerary of President McKinley's visit to the Expo:

8:15 a.m.—Leave the Milburn home.

11:15 a.m.—Arrive at Niagara Falls.

12:05 p.m.—Luncheon at the International Hotel.

2:00 p.m.—Tour of Niagara Power House.

4:00 p.m.—Arrive at the Temple of Music for public reception.

4:07 p.m.   *He said he waited in line, that he had placed the revolver in his right hand and had covered it with a handkerchief, and that he put the hand and revolver in his right-hand pocket and kept it there until he came to the place in the Temple of Music where the crowds were sifted into single file. Then he took the revolver, concealed under the handkerchief, from his pocket and held his hand across his stomach and, when he was opposite the President, he fired the shots.*

In the Temple of Music, the Coward Leon Czolgosz was immediately thrown to the ground, disarmed, and choked by the six-foot-six waiter who stood behind him in the presidential receiving line. Another bystander restrained him, and as a Secret Service agent pulled him from the temple, he punched Czolgosz hard in the face until he bled. After trial, Czolgosz arrived at the Auburn Prison having been ransacked by the mobs of angry New Yorkers that awaited him on the train platforms. His clothes were in tatters and he could barely walk by the time he landed in his cell.

The lamps in the Expo's emergency hospital were so poor, surgery aides had to hold a mirror over the president to catch the light of the sun. An X-ray machine the Edison laboratories spent four years developing was on display at the fair, so an engineer rushed it from the Midway to the house where McKinley rested. They found a fairgoer of the president's size to sit under a half-hour of electric fluorescence, and the X-ray successfully detected a nickel under the man's back. It might have found the bullet lost in McKinley's abdomen, had the wary medical team trusted the newfangled electric machine.

The Edison Studios film, dated September 15, is called *President McKinley's Funeral Cortege at Buffalo, NY*. It's seven minutes long and begins with a military band marching at half-time, instruments lowered. A long color guard follows, and then rows upon rows of soldiers. Then Boy Scouts. Then three carriages pulled by two horses each. Finally, the casket, in a carriage with glass doors, pulled by four dark horses. When the flower-strewn casket is lifted out, the men remove their hats, despite the fact that it's pouring.

September 30, in the photo-series *Shots on the Midway*:

> *There is a boxing kangaroo of almost human intelligence and sometimes more than human precision. And latterly the largest*

elephant in captivity, Jumbo II, late of his Majesty's service in India, man-eater and howdah carrier, a walking mountain that weighs nine tons.

October 29, in the *Buffalo Evening News*:

At 7:12:30 o'clock this morning Leon Czolgosz, murderer of President McKinley, paid the extreme penalty exacted by the law for his crime. He was shocked to death by 1,700 volts of electricity. He went to the chair in exactly the same manner as have the majority of all the other murderers in this State, showing no particular sign of fear but, in fact, doing what few of them have done, talking to the witnesses while he was being strapped in the chair.

"I killed the President because he was an enemy of the good people—of the good working people. I am not sorry for my crime."

In the last week of the fair, Jumbo II was said to have gone ugly from the close quarters backstage at Bostock's Arena. The *Buffalo Daily Courier* reported he tried to kill two of his keepers with his trunk, breaking Charles Miller's arm and sending Henry Mullen to the hospital with multiple injuries. Bostock said the men would have died, had Jumbo II's legs not been so tightly chained.

The last straw was either when Jumbo II (reportedly) took a swing at the eleven-year-old daughter of a Midway vendor or when he (reportedly) took a swing at Bostock himself.

The Expo was not nearly as lucrative as "The Animal King" had anticipated, what with the rain, high winds, assassinations, etc. His star human act, four-foot-tall Chiquita the Doll Lady, had just run off with a ticket-taker and was suing him for twenty thousand dollars. Bostock made it known that he was in no mood to fool with an ugly elephant.

November 2, in the *Buffalo Evening News*:
> *The Pan-American Exposition is ended. At midnight Exposition President Milburn touched an electric button, connected by wires with the rheostat and causing the 160,000 incandescent lights in the grounds to darken forever. The ceremonies were simple but solemn in the extreme.*

> *The death of the Exposition was apparently painless.*

One unforeseen side effect of concluding the Expo—of dimming the magic it made—was an all-out riot. Late into "Buffalo Day," the closing festivities of singing, dancing, and running to Bostock's Arena to tease the camels and elephants escalated into breaking windows and tearing down statues. The mob smashed every light bulb they could onto the bricks of the Midway. Hooligans uprooted yards of landscaping to make switches, which they used to slap women in the face—extra points if the dollies bled. Rioters of both sexes choked one another with fistfuls of fallen confetti.

On November 3, the *Buffalo Evening News* estimated ten thousand contributed to the chaos:
> *None of the insane patients in the State Hospital escaped to the Pan-American Exposition on Saturday night, but judging by the wanton vandalism that ran riot there, it would be hard to explain it on any other score than that a hundred or more maniacs had been busy in the neighborhood.*

> *The place looked as if a herd of huge elephants had stampeded through it.*

On November 4, the debris from the riots still clogged the Midway when Frank Bostock announced the Expo's *true* finale would be the death of an ugly elephant, at 2:30 p.m., *most likely hanged or choked with chains*. Tickets were set at a half-dollar, discounted for minors. The Expo's train station scheduled extra arrivals. Buffalo's officials begged Bostock to reconsider.

That same day, in the *Wilkes-Barre Times*: *UNEXPECTED PER-FORMANCE ON THE BUFFALO MIDWAY*.

The Edison Studios' *Execution of Czolgosz with Panorama of Auburn Prison* wasn't finished until eleven days after the assassin's death. The film is half real, half humbug. It shows live, execution-day footage of the prison exterior in the opening shot, the same jail that electro-cuted the first man in history and Westinghoused dozens more until all state-sanctioned deaths were sent to New York's other electric chair—Sing Sing's "Old Sparky"—in 1914. Those trees in the opening shot are the very trees the men and boys climbed that same day to see if a view of the Czolgosz death was possible.

But after this panoramic shot, the camera cuts to a brick-walled room, filmed not at Auburn, but with actors at Edison's Manhattan studios, just three miles from the Pearl Street neighborhood Edison had electrified twenty years before.

The fake guards quickly strap the fake assassin in the chair, all four of them buckling, attaching. The actor playing Czolgosz—Czolgosz II, if you will—is blindfolded, where the real Czolgosz wore a hood-cap in his final minutes. An official-looking man raises a finger and each time he does, an actor in the doorway mimes throwing a switch with his upstage hand. Czolgosz II inhales at the 1,700 volts of alternating current (not) moving through him, then braces himself into a higher sitting position. At the second sham jolt, he leans forward slightly, as if riding downhill.

Jumbo II's punishment began as water, moving a few miles upstream from the Falls. At the bottom of a canal that men had dug into the Niagara river, five-foot wheels turned in the liquid current. Their motion powered the twenty-one dynamos of the limestone powerhouse, and that energy morphed the liquid current into lightning. This moved through transformers that bolstered it into layered waves—2,200 alternating volts of them. In transmission cables the diameter of jelly jars, the lightning ran thirty miles inland to the dismantling fair, into the loud arena, where the Animal King turned to his elephant.

November 11,
in the *Fort Worth Morning Register*:   DID NOT KILL HIM
in the *Kansas City Star*:   COULDN'T KILL THE
    ELEPHANT
in the *Kalamazoo Gazette*:   JUMBO II STILL LIVES
in the *San Francisco Call*:   TWO THOUSAND TWO
    HUNDRED ELECTRIC
    VOLTS FAIL TO KILL
    JUMBO AT EXPOSITION:

Jumbo was chained to a plank platform. Electrodes the size of a large sponge were placed behind his ears and at the end of his spinal column. Only 2,200 volts had been provided for by those in charge. The shock was repeated six times. Jumbo wagged his tail, tore up a plank with his trunk, looked pleased and trumpeted a bit. The shocks had simply tickled him. Jumbo merely threw a trunkful of dirt over his back and refused to die.

After the unsuccessful attempt to kill him, Jumbo was unhitched from his harness. When led back to his quarters the elephant was none the worse for his electric bath.

Explanations made by the electricians for the failure were that Jumbo's hide had the resistance of rubber and that this formed a non-conductor Impervious to electricity. Others declare that if it takes 1,800 volts to kill a man, it would necessarily take more than 2,200 volts to kill an elephant.

On November 17, the *Charlotte Observer* reported that Bostock was now in talks to send the disgraced Jumbo II to a bullfighting promoter in Mexico. The last recorded use of a bullfight to execute an elephant was nearly two thousand years before, in the Roman Colosseum. Instead, Jumbo II remained in the states, soon shipped to a creditor in Manhattan Beach, Ohio. Bostock's other elephant was sent to Coney Island, along with the Expo's world-famous carnival "dark ride," A Trip to the Moon.

At the close of the first year of the new century, a tiger tore off Frank Bostock's right arm while the man was saving a female performer from getting mauled. When asked about it, Bostock told the press the tiger was not to blame.

1903

Though his name is listed on the title card of every Kinetoscope movie, it's unlikely Edison had much to do with the short films of Edison Studios. The War of Currents was basically over and alternating current had triumphed, so it's possible he had no clue about the plans to make *Electrocuting an Elephant*. The film is a minute-long, live short of the first elephant—and the second female of any species on the planet—to be condemned to electrocution for her crimes.

In the yards around Coney Island's Luna Park, the condemned elephant places each foot onto a copper plate. Once ignited with over 6,000 volts of alternating current, they smoke beneath her planted feet. The smoke rises around her body, her trunk goes rigid, and all five tons of her list forward.

In her youth, America had called her "The Baby Elephant"— another in a long line of animals with the same adorable, temporary name.

June 25, in the *New York Times: TWIN ELEPHANTS BORN:*
> *to Big Liz, the only female elephant in Bostock's collection at Sea Beach Palace, Coney Island. One of the twins lived only a short time, but the other will probably survive.*

> *The twins were born between 4 and 4:30 p.m. in the stall which Big Liz regularly occupies. A wall of canvas was at once erected about them. The babies were directly named Shamrock III and Reliance. It was Reliance that died.*

> *The father of the babies is Jumbo II, whom Liz met at the Pan-American Exposition twenty-two months ago. It is said that Jumbo II is at the present time dying of blood poisoning in Cleveland, Ohio.*

And November 29, in *Billboard*, some of which is probably true:
> *Jumbo II, the big elephant belonging to Bostock, which had been left behind at Manhattan Beach, Cleveland, O., last summer, on account of a creditor's attachment, is no more.*

> *About a week ago he showed signs of sickness.*

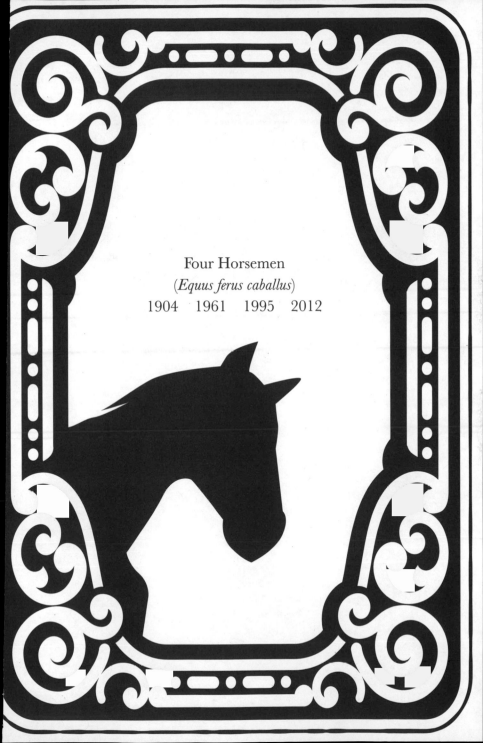

Four Horsemen
(*Equus ferus caballus*)
1904   1961   1995   2012

WILBUR: I just don't understand it!
ED: Don't try to. It's bigger than both of us.

CLEVER HANS

According to Herr von Osten, it began with a kitten, a bear cub, and a horse. The retired teacher spent weeks grabbing their furry appendages and tapping them on the courtyard floor *one-two-three*, while saying the numbers aloud—*one-two-three, one-two-three*—hoping something might stick in an animal's brain. The kitten and bear were useless, but the horse seemed to figure it out.

Hans learned to tap his right hoof *one-two-three*, then to double *one-two-three* on command by tapping six times, then to subtract five and tap only the *one*. Then, with the epic patience reserved for a wayward schoolboy, Herr von Osten went further. It took years, but he taught the horse fractions, then decimal places, then colors and days of the week. The alphabet as permutations of taps on a special handmade platform box. Tones in the musical scale as taps. Tapping the differences between straw hats and felt ones, and scores of other human practices rarely shared with "the lower forms."

Soon, his North Berlin courtyard was packed every noon-time. Gentlemen on lunch breaks, truant delivery boys, and ladies shaded by parasols all squeezed close to the tall Orlov Trotter, with Herr von Osten nearby in his long coat and slouch hat. He often prompted onlookers to question the horse themselves, reminding them their inquiries must be gently voiced:

What are the factors of forty-nine?

If the third day of the month comes on a Wednesday, what day and date is a fortnight after?

Is this a pleasing chord? No? Then which tone should I omit?

I'm thinking of a number. If I subtract four from it, I have eighteen. What number is in my mind?

A state-sanctioned posse of zoologists, viscounts, and circus men came to the courtyard to debunk the act, but they debunked nothing. By then, the world was watching; papers in Europe and all the way to North America ran the story of "BERLIN'S WON-DERFUL HORSE: He Can Do Almost Anything but Talk." Even the Hans Commission's circus pro, who knew a thing or two about trick horses, confessed his shock. Herr Von Osten, they agreed, was an honest horseman; their poking around Hans revealed no sign of fraud. They told the papers that the nine-year-old gelding must have the brain of a twelve-year-old human child.

In the very distant past, when our world was unrecognizable, human and horse brains matched. We don't know exactly when this was—somewhere in a span of about thirty-four million years—but once upon a time, we were identical: small, ratlike, and vertebrate, with sharp mouths and sensitive eyes, thinking as one, hiding in the underbrush of our strange and green planet from the giant beasts that owned it. And then an asteroid hit, almost everybody died, the lush green became mottled with fruits and flowers, and as we ate them, our bodies changed. We slunk out from the underbrush and became many creatures, each one lost in its own thoughts.

The psychologist on the Hans Commission sent one of his lab assistants, named Herr Pfungst, back to the courtyard for more exhaustive trials. Herr Pfungst erected a tent and banished the crowds; eventually, he banished Herr von Osten, too. He blinkered Hans, deafened him, plugged his nose, and asked him backward questions. It took months, but the man finally found a pattern. If Hans couldn't see his interrogator, he couldn't answer correctly. The horse would search for the voice asking the question, chew the air, and then give his default response of *one-two-three*. Other times he'd just keep tapping the hoof-box like an uncertain metronome. Herr Pfungst discovered that if the question was rigged so the human could ask it without knowing the answer, the horse always tapped incorrectly. There was something about the human knowing—the fact of the answer planted inside the human brain—that Hans understood.

For years, the horse had watched the human bodies in the courtyard clench and lean. From the inside out, they tightened as the magic number of taps approached, and they relaxed upon hearing it. Then a carrot for Hans, a hunk of bread, or a sugar lump, and—though it never seemed to matter much to him—a round of applause. Herr Von Osten's meticulousness hadn't taught Hans algebra or words; it taught him the secret languages of the bodies who anxiously watched over him. Here is what Hans actually learned: hoof-tapping brought reward only if he could read the minute tensions a human body holds while it awaits satisfaction.

In his trials, Pfungst found he could rig himself to cue Hans for the wrong answers. He'd ask the horse *what is twelve times three?* and then concentrate on the number twenty-eight with all his might. He'd focus on Hans's tapping hooves with that wrong number center stage in his mind—fooling himself, letting himself hope and then trust the horse was traveling toward the incorrect answer inside him.

But when a man puts a burning number twenty-eight in his brain and bears down on it with all his heart—until a horse can read it in his fists, breath, face, and feet—how could that number possibly be incorrect?

•• ▬ • ▬ ••

BAMBOO HARVESTER

The animal from the first pilot episode was a tawny quarter horse with a hard mouth and little interest in new tricks. After that pilot flopped, Filmways Studios replaced nearly everything for the re-shoot: a goofier Wilbur, a blonder wife, a different last name, and a brand new horse. Palomino this time—like Trigger!—and not a rental, either.

They searched four states to find him. Within two weeks of purchase, he'd been gelded and registered in his new name. It was less of a mouthful than "Bamboo Harvester" and much more Horse Next Door—perfect for prime time, 1961. He cost the studio fifteen hundred dollars. You bet your ass they checked his teeth first.

The equine mouth is full of facts; that's why you don't look a gift horse there. You might as well treat it like a price tag, because age, care, diet, temperament—they all come straight from the horse's mouth. The grooves of the molars show what he has chewed: oats or grain or sandy weeds pulled from hard ground-cover. A dark streak at the gum line would confess he was past his prime, and a run of "cups" on the tooth-ridges would report his prematurity. Well-filed molars meant he'd been handled with care.

Beyond that, the horse's mouth tells a ten-million-year story of triumph. Epochs built that mouth, as the planet morphed from Eocene to Oligocene to Miocene and took horses with it. When the earth cooled and jungles gave way to steppes, the horse mouth stretched to accommodate snippy, foraging incisors at the front and a factory of molars in the back. This pushed the eye up toward the ears and yielded that famous long face. Those back teeth let digestion begin in the mouth, a key to quick energy and amped-up thought, and they allowed the frontal lobe to swell, upping facial sensitivity. One of the great marvels of mammalian biology, soon to be seen grinning on the cover of *TV Guide*.

Mister Ed picks up the telephone to call Clint Eastwood. Mister Ed wields a paddle to whup Wilbur at Ping-Pong. Mister Ed reels in a fish, types his memoirs, bowls a perfect game, swipes Wilbur's wallet, emancipates a cockatiel, kisses his reflection, and sings the hit song, "Pretty Little Filly with the Ponytail"—all with his fabulous mouth. And of course, Mister Ed talks.

His fourth line in the reshot pilot is "How now, brown cow"— wordplay meant to strike some barnyard resonance—but no bovine could handle that tongue twister, because a cow's mouth can't rise to any challenges. Where cows use lips mostly as protective cases for teeth, horse lips are much more ambitious. Six long muscles pull in multiple directions. The upper lip is prehensile and almost frighteningly sensitive, designed not only to grab food, but to sort it. As their mouths became nimbler, horses developed culture around their lips, which became velvety social instruments for nipping and nuzzling and holding emotional tension. So much of horse culture depends on these genius mouths.

That old yarn about Ed's trainer smearing peanut butter on the horse's gums is a half-truth at best, and the rumor that they stuck an electric prod up his ass? Also bull. Most signs point to the use of a clear nylon line strung under Mister Ed's lip that, when given a signal, he'd work to remove. At another signal (a crop tapped on a rear pastern, perhaps), he'd shut his mouth. Or at least that's how it went for the first few dozen episodes, until the horse— ever sensitive to the commands of his crowd—evolved.

There's a visible difference in Mister Ed's talking between the first two seasons. Early on, it's much broader; he opens wide, reaches toward Wilbur with his tongue, and jaws his lines. As the episodes progress, however, Ed minimizes the movement, keeping his teeth closed and just wiggling his lips. The B-movie cowboy who provided Ed's voice didn't alter his drawl one bit, though.

This smaller talking could happen without strings, as the horse could now respond to the touch-signal alone. And by the end of the show's five-year run, he didn't even need the crop. He'd figured out they wanted him to lip-wiggle whenever he was alone with Wilbur, after Wilbur stopped speaking.

In 1994, Alan Young, the actor who played Wilbur, published his life story, which was at least fifty percent Ed stories. "Despite my early doubts," Young writes, "working with a horse turned out to be the joy of my life." He remembers taking horseback rides around the lots with the trainer who kept Ed. As Young chatted in the saddle, the trainer noticed Ed plodding along below him. Free and away from any cameras, the horse would still move his lips whenever the man on his back fell silent.

•• ▬ • ▬ ••

EASTERN EXPRESS

No backbone on earth is more rideable than the spine that gallops beneath you. It outnumbers yours by six thoracic vertebrae, all of which have ossified into a firm and sturdy line with a network of sinew supporting it. Behind you is where the gallop generates; this rear placement keeps the back more balanced than any ass or bull or camel. The legs beneath the hips and shoulders spent fifty million years growing long enough for this work. That's what separates the spine you're riding from the planet's shorter quadrupeds, which must put their backs into running. And it's also unlike *you*, with your lopsided limbs, soft feet, low endurance, and brittle neckbone.

Add to this eighteen hundred years of saddles over that spine, seventeen centuries of stirrups, three millennia of bridles, and five thousand years of slowly showing a horse how you might sit on his back. Plus the years you've spent getting this particular body, this fused horse-and-rider, to gallop courses—like the one that stretches in front of you right now—in your spooky, thrilling tandem.

For this course is not the perpendicular ride of trail pony and tourist. You're no cowboy fighting with one arm against a hell-bent bronco. This ride is a language—each connecting point between you is a word. As he runs, your legs speak to his belly and backside, your hips and butt press to keep him supported; your hands help his neck rise and reach. The combinations of signals at varied intensities make these body-words into phrases, sentences even. And this six-minute run through changeable terrain is like two miles of free-written paragraphs, composed over mud and hedges and fences and ponds at twenty-one miles an hour.

He's never run this course before, never even walked it, as per the event's rules. His trust in you is what sends him barreling toward a four-foot jump, reading your movements as fast as you can execute them. Moments before a jump, in the crucial last steps leading to the launch, you'll discard him if you hinge forward into your jumping stance too early. Though crucial to give him momentum, that jump position is at his neck, and it's like going off-line. It's a blackout at Mission Control, a trapeze man tossing his partner before she sees the bar. Get into the pose too early, and the event's judges will say you've "thrown the horse away."

A thrown-away horse might just stop moving, which rockets his lifted rider between his ears like a football through a goalpost. So keep your legs and hips and hands where he can feel them for as long as possible, sitz bones all but touching the saddle and calibrating with his every step. Lots of leg as he looks for the fences, a position that tells him, *I'm still here; I know what's coming.* His ears prick forward when he finally sees the jump, but even then, careful still. Count your strides. Leg on. Stay with him, over his back.

Because all around you, people are falling from horses: a third of the field eliminated after botching the width of a fence, or popping loose from the saddle on a slope. They call the course ditches "coffins" for the many horses they've spooked. When they end up separated, on either side of a tall fence, a horse and its human often call out to one another, using their voices to rejoin.

But you knew your first day on a horse that you'd spend years hitting the ground. It's a fact that never disappears, and what more can you expect when you jump on a thousand-pound flight animal and ask it to run with all its might? It's an insane prospect, but the reward is equally nuts. A man cannot fly without proportionate risk—which you, of all people, should know.

Of course you won't know any of this at the time. You'll remember nothing of the run at all. The last thing you'll recall is chatting at the stables about the sweet, hungry horse you've been working up the levels, with his silly, inherited barn-name of "Bucket" that you've since shortened to "Buck." A misnomer for such a gentle, eager guy that, unlike the feistier rides of your past, keeps you sturdy—as long as you don't find a way to fuck things up.

You won't remember the starting box and the slight tension in his back from the dressage round, or cantering out of the box to your first little jump. You won't remember the second obstacle, or your approach to the third—an easy "filler fence" just meant to establish rhythm—and you certainly won't remember that awful choice to raise your body from his a half-stride too soon, disappearing from him, up into his neck.

He has seven neck vertebrae, just like you do, named the same as yours, and you'll roll forward over all of them, still holding onto the reins and taking the bridle with you. Past his axis vertebra, which rotates his head, just as yours does, and his atlas bone, which, like yours, supports the skull and holds the brainstem.

In your own neck, these two bones will bear the full weight of your fall, all six-plus feet of you down seventeen hands of horse. The feet and hands of a fused body are now split back in two. Two spines: one chuffing on the other side of the little fence, the other sputtering "I can't breathe" and fighting the medics like a cagey pony. With each twitch of your head, bone shards puncture your spinal cord.

The crowd will come closer, saying your name, for they all know who you are; the cameras had come along (of course) because they heard you were in town, and you'll just be on the ground there, not moving at all anymore, your neck at this odd angle. You who'd just looked so smooth for the cameras atop another huge, magnificent creature—another shiny star; you rode together so mightily, like a confident, superhuman thing; and now the horse is back in the barn—who knows what Buck can remember—and you're blacked out and flying without him, up, up and away in a medevac copter named, of all goddamned things, Pegasus.

•• ▬ • ▬ ••

OREO

An overturned horse is a sickly lurch in the human gut. Something about that body twisted—robbed of the grace we demand from it—nauseates. All that flesh is, to us, a landscape in peril, which perhaps explains the countless fallen horses of art. See the contorted necks of Delacroix, the lolling tongues of Hogarth, the chariot-flattened bodies of the *Alexander Mosaic*.

And we cannot forget the eyes of the screaming horse in the middle of *Guernica*. Just two dots in two wobbly circles, but still the exact, maddening idea of a horse crazed with fear. Picasso's horse eyes, turned backward in the figure's wrenched neck, are what set the whole painting spinning.

At 4:20 p.m., a scaffold clanged to the pavement in front of his carriage, and Oreo just bolted. His driver still held the reins, so the horse dragged the buggy into Columbus Circle. When he hit a parked BMW, the back half of the carriage ripped off with a pair of Australian tourists still aboard. Several blocks north, the rest of it broke free, and the unhindered horse careened down Ninth Avenue, crossing Fifty-Ninth, Fifty-Eighth, and then, suddenly, halting. The bystanders who yelled after him said Oreo stopped at Fifty-Seventh Street when he saw the red traffic light.

There is no larger mammal eye on dry land than that of *Equus ferus caballus*. Gigantic and roving, it magnifies objects much larger than human eyes do. From the sides of the head, a horse eye sees almost all the way behind its body. Even when the horse stoops to graze, the eyes scan the world for reasons to flee. While human eyes evolved into sharp, forward-facing, and predatory things, the horse eye grew to want the big picture—just enough to spot the shadow of risk and then take off running with its mighty body. The horse eye is hardwired for surprise, and the horse body spring-loaded to obey the eye's command. Fear, as embodied in the eyeball, is what keeps a horse alive.

By 4:35 two men had led Oreo to the sidewalk and tied him to a pole and a tree. He was still wearing his blinkers, so he had no sense of what was behind him or to his left and right. The blinkers were meant as a reassurance—to keep him calm and forward-focused while he worked. A horse's vision is so broad and sensitive, even the carriage he pulls can startle him. But now the carriage was gone, as was his driver, and he was alone on the street with access to less than twenty-five percent of his natural vision.

"He's so stressed," muttered a deep voice near a camera phone.

By the time the mounted police managed to shoot him with a mild tranquilizer, a crowd had formed, fixated on the horse as he shook loose his livery, fought the dart, and bared his teeth. His eyes rolled in his head and he wouldn't stop licking the air.

At a moment of horse-panic, the eyes appear to bulge, thanks to a system of muscles under the skin that expands, like a camera aperture forced open. Though terrified, the body tells the horse to look harder. As the eyes dart and roll, the white sclera around the iris becomes further pronounced. The new white makes them more like our own eyes, with their constant pearlescent frames. Perhaps we're so moved to paint or sculpt a horse's frightened eye because it best resembles our own.

At 4:40, the drugs kicked in and took Oreo's fear away from him. He lowered his top half, front knees bent but back legs kept straight, like a cat after a nap. From there, swaying a bit, he twisted until his back legs gave out beneath him. When his rump finally hit the black street, the crowd's reaction was audible—a chorus of *ohhhh*s as Oreo curved into himself.

"Once they go down, they hit," the same deep voice said, which didn't help anyone.

"Look at that," a higher voice said, which is perhaps closer to the point.

Look at that. Look at the body on the pavement, that eye growing all-brown and still. After five thousand years of shading the horse from fear (for our own interests), we still cannot conquer it for him. We've spent fifty-six million years swallowing our human fear, but his whole body still revolves around it. Fear is the lens with which a horse sees the world; it's moved him over six continents. Not the grace or power or intelligence we claim to prize in him, but this primordial fear, as old as either species. And if we've been close to his fear all this time, what did we do with our own?

Look at him looking. Look at him searching us. What does this giant eye, set upon us for so very long, see that we still cannot?

See the frightened kid who mistakes the gaze of six horses for God's judgment, and then blinds them. See the apocalyptic visions in which the Lord swears to "strike every horse with panic" and "keep a watchful eye over Judah, but . . . blind the horses of the nations."

See the old Grimms' tale of Clever Hans, who gouges every horse eye in his stable and then throws them into the lap of his beloved when she asks the dim boy to "cast a friendly eye" upon her. When she sees that she's covered in the eyes of Hans's horses, the beloved panics and takes off running.

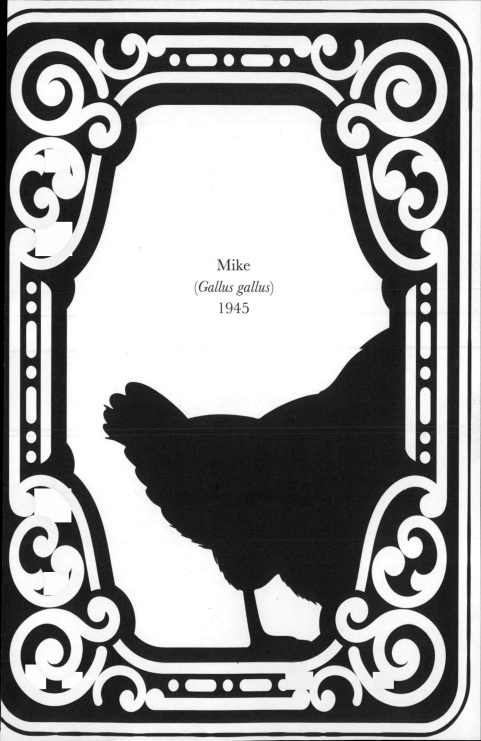

Mike
(*Gallus gallus*)
1945

Human society, like Mike, is getting by on its resources.

Time, October 29, 1945

M IKE QUICKLY FIGURED OUT HE could no longer crow. The few times he attempted to—hunkering into a center-stage chicken squat and flexing his wings—he only managed a low rumble in his belly. It felt like being buried under a mound of mud. It sounded like a kitchen sink with drain trouble. The gurgle and choke made Oley run for the eyedropper to squeeze Mike's clogged neck-hole clear.

A shame, thought Oley and Clara. They could've upped the admission at least a dime for crowing. I mean, look how the crowds clamored when Mike gave 'em the littlest wing flap. But charging more than a quarter for a bird that mostly sat there just wasn't Christian, head or no head. Plus, the show already ran on sin; that head in the Mason jar next to Mike was bogus. Back home in Fruita, Colorado, Clara's tabby had run away with Mike's God-given head, so Oley pickled a decoy to take on the road.

The newshounds came out to Fruita with their notepads, as did the zoological types with their magnifying lenses. They ate up

Clara's gravy pie and gawked at Mike's spared brain stem and filed their stories from the field: "Beheaded Chicken Calmly Lives On" and "Headless Chicken Alive and Gaining Weight." After the mentions in *Life* and the Guinness Book and the all-expenses-paid trip to the lab in Salt Lake—around the time tongues were wagging about Oley's new-bought hay baler and his fresh-off-the-lot Chevy pickup—another rumor must've brewed that Fruita water helped chicken blood clot. After that, you couldn't swing an axe without hitting some Fruitan who'd pinned down his own Wyandotte, first squinting himself as cockeyed as they imagined Oley to be. They'd miss the opening stroke on purpose to heat the blade, then they'd slice through the hackle feathers at a diagonal, sparing the base of the neck, where most of the chicken-brain hunkers low in a corner. Then the family would watch as the rooster's head rolled.

The birds usually staggered off the blocks and stepped—one, two, three—before toppling into the dirt. A few stayed alive for the afternoon, or past sundown, or maybe even into the next day—the whole farm white-knuckled and unblinking until the birds bled out, or bashed into the stovepipe, or fell off the porch, or something. Mike could've told them: staying alive without a head is tricky.

The old men at Fruita's Monument Café went on record that they couldn't care less. Outside the Monument, though, the little girls with jump ropes demanded answers: "Mike, Mike, where is your head? Even without it, you aren't dead!" One article answered the girls, saying Mike wasn't dead because his will to live was "almost human." But where in a headless chicken does this almost-human willpower lie? Nobody thought to ask that, and Mike obviously wasn't talking.

It can't live in his cocksureness, since crowing was off limits and his gone head scared the hens away. Could the will be vascular, then? A coagulative will? The simple will of platelets, thrombin, and myelin to keep godlessly plugging and sheathing? Or could Mike have the same will of those brachiosaur bones hanging tough in the Fruita shale, waiting for their second acts as hair combs, figurines—curios you have to be careful not to break while dusting the mantel?

He could have willed himself to fight the sure thing that is human folly, a noble course for any animal in the kingdom. Perhaps he already knew, that sharp night on the block, that Clara's mother was visiting and making Oley's axe hand anxious. He couldn't help but reckon that, at some point, Oley would let that head-thieving cat out of his sights. He probably bet his bottom chicken dollar that one of these evenings, after the show, in one of these dank motor inns, he'd choke up, only to learn that Oley had left his crucial eyedropper at the last tour stop, two hundred miles in the dust.

What if Mike stayed alive, ghost head shaking in disgust, just to see what those two would cock up next?

But perhaps it's best for all involved to think that Mike's will was something else altogether. Some living things harbor another nervous system—one that pushes them past simply crowing, past just chasing hens, and even past the natural order. What's the harm, really, in saying that Mike stayed alive for the promise of a tiny tent twisting with reverb? Or for cheers so loud he could feel them in the bumps of his skin? For the good burn of hot lights sizzling with moth wings, Clara's starstruck touch on his back, or the soft fuzz of a hotel blanket in place of chicken wire and an apple box. For fan mail simply addressed to "the Headless Chicken in Colorado" that the post office knew to deliver to Mike's farm.

Let's tell ourselves *this* was what pushed him forward—eighteen months past one final lap around the yard and a headless roast. Maybe that same will to remain a rooster for five hundred unseen sun-ups is the will of Ziegfeld, of flash bulbs, of Borscht

Belts, of gotta-dance. Of *take my hen, please, (badump bump)* and *"Doc, my head hurts when I do this!" "Well, then you better not do that,"(badump bump)* and *Momma always said don't count your chickens before they're axed, (badump bump)* and *Rooster? I barely know 'er! (badump bump)*.

Maybe Mike always knew that, in this world, baby? You're gonna need a gimmick if you truly wanna get ahead.

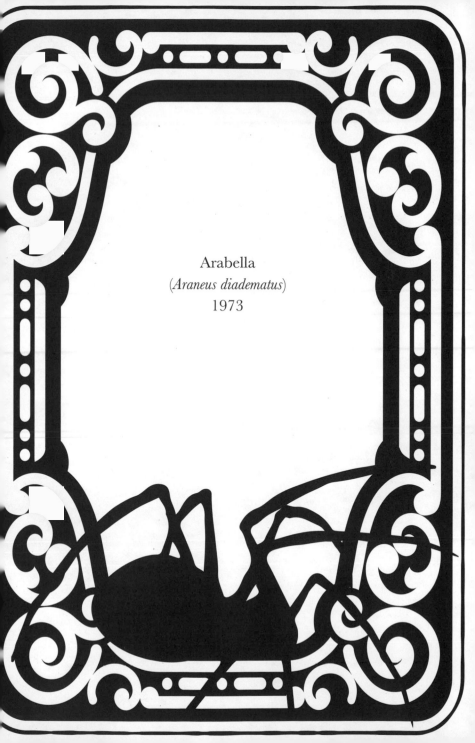

Arabella
(*Araneus diadematus*)
1973

The tiny insect had, in many ways, been Skylab's star performer.

Reuters

IN EARLY SUMMER, ONCE SHE has broken from her cocoon and spent a day or so in the huddle of her family, an adolescent cross spider feels ready to fly. She scuttles to some swatch of vegetation that faces outward—a leaf ridge, a twig—and she perches there. Then she lifts a significant fraction of her legs and pulls a silk strand from the spinnerets at the base of her abdomen. Ounce for ounce, that silk is five times the strength of reinforced steel and at least twice as strong as a human femur.

When a June wind blows the silk strand into its current, she follows it with her body: a tiny balloon chasing its string. It is a journey that begins with a considerable jerk and ends only when her silk tether collides with a rooted object—a bush, a fencepost. This could be a one-yard trip, or it could send her half a mile away. A half-mile journey to a cross spider is like a man catching a wind from Milwaukee to Madison.

Gravity left the bodies of the Skylab III crew without much warning. They had spent the early minutes of the launch pressed down into their command module's "couch" while 7.7 million pounds of rocket thrust pushed away the Earth. Now, a small space separated their thighs from the seat fabric. If not for the straps of their harnesses, the three men would have risen like milkweed to the low ceilings of the transport pod.

It would be several more hours before a dot appeared in the navigational telescope, unmistakably white against the black of space. More hours still, waiting and hovering, until the dot became a shining oblong cylinder, flanked by two giant solar-paneled flags and topped with a windmill-shaped telescope. Skylab. Here was where they would dock themselves: at the gate of this white and black and brilliant gold capsule, which was falling in the orbit of the planet they'd escaped at nearly one half mile per second.

Not too long after landing, a cross spider spins her first full web. She casts a line outward, waits to feel it catch, and then secures the other end of the line to the spot where she rests. This creates a single-strand bridge that she can walk across, which she does, reinforcing it with a second bridge-line. Once suspended from the center of that bridge, she free-falls, still pumping silk to form a Y-shape. She then pulls strand after strand from her body, spinning and falling, climbing and plummeting, hooking each strand to the crotch of that Y. Soon, a dozen spokes branch from the Y-hub like a silken sunburst.

Without stopping, she turns sideways and circles the spokes, connecting them in thirty cartwheeled spirals. Here is when she switches the gears of her body to produce a stickier silk—viscid enough to trap heavy prey. With this silk she weaves a second spiral. After that's done, she eats the first spiral, then she eats the hub, and finally she arranges herself in the hub's place. And though she will never rate a vantage to see her handiwork (even if she could, her eyes can't focus at such a distance), the young spider has just filled her space with one of our Earth's most spectacular pieces of craftsmanship, just as versions of herself have done for hundreds of millions of years. It takes her about half an hour.

NASA spent almost a decade designing Skylab's orbital workshop, and its final blueprint held limited consideration for up and down. Rather than separate the station's two levels with a solid floor, a crosshatching of beams split the workshop like an open, metallic net. A long blue pole ran through the center, so the men could pull themselves along the workshop's forty-eight feet, but the astronauts scrapped the pole shortly after getting their space bearings. They preferred pushing off the walls and steering with their arms, floating through that empty center to travel from the workshop's fore level—site of the dinner table, the latrine, and the three booths in which they slept bolted to the walls—to the aft level—with its radio and TV equipment, its biophysics lab, its materials processors, and its plastic vial the size of a human thumb containing a young cross spider named Arabella.

A spider was built to strum her web like a guitar. She was built to pluck a radial with one striped tarsal claw and feel how the pull of the world changes the vibration of her web. She was built to spin more sticky strands at web-bottom than at web-top, as gravity makes jumping down to prey less taxing than climbing up to it. She was built to drop a gossamer line and free-fall from danger, to walk the strands of her handiwork upside down, using her weight for propulsion.

For nothing says "spider" more than this built-in vigilance, this innate knowledge of what pushes her into the earth and what lifts her away from it. Her legs, claws, mouth, the silk she unspools from inside herself, they all understand—with the hair-trigger sensitivity that comes from eons of experiments—the facts of our massive planet trying to collide with her body.

•• •• •• •

It wasn't until the eighth day of the mission that Science Pilot Owen Garriott floated over to Arabella's little vial. NASA had custom-built her a fifteen-inch square cage, as narrow as a framed portrait, with a flat glass front. Around the frame were mounts for long fluorescent bulbs and cameras, and at the top right corner was an attachment point for Arabella's transport vial, which would create a narrow tunnel for her to pass into the cage. Nobody wanted to risk releasing a tiny spider into the free space of the orbital workshop, which the crew knew had a mind of its own.

She refused to take the tunnel for a full mission day. Though she was only the responsibility of the science pilot, the two other crewmen couldn't help but keep tabs on her. Pilot Jack Lousma watched Garriott opening Arabella's vial and floated over to assist. "It didn't know where it was, poor spider," he later remembered. Commander Alan Bean, one of the dozen men who have walked on the moon, noted her in his private journal: "Owen got the vial off the cage, opened the door, and shook her out, where she immediately bounced back and forth, front to back, four or five times, then locked onto the screen panels at the box edge. There she sits, clutching the screen."

The sixteen-millimeter film of Arabella's earliest work on Skylab depicts not so much a spider as the specter of one—a black-and-grey arachno-ghost. Eight thin strands glimmer about her body: these are her legs. White dots sparkle from a dozen other faint pinstripes: these are her gossamer. In the film, she tries to free-fall and hang an early radial, with tumultuous results. You see her scurry along a horizontal line, half holding on and half bouncing, until she loses all footing; then weightlessness floats her above the line. A flailing of legs sends her tumbling in the other direction, sinking lower, though there is no "lower" to a spider somersaulting in a cage-in-space. She first flips head over abdomen, then corkscrews, so that her rolling turns sideways. Her legs reach outward in eight directions; then they all move inward, clutching the empty space as one desperate claw. Eventually, she finds the hard purchase of the cage's corner, and tries to locate some stillness there.

Science Pilot Garriott had spent months rehearsing his upcoming spacewalks on a drowned Skylab mock-up in Huntsville. On Mission Day 9, he shut the airlock room off to the rest of the station, opened the execution hatch, and exited to a place only twenty-five men had gone before him: out into the thermosphere, the "hard vacuum," the emptiness between the Earth and its closest celestial neighbor. A sixty-foot cord spooled out from his abdomen.

Slowed by the fat fingers of his gloves, he was surprised by the effort it took to pull a five-foot pole of thin steel from the hatch, then another, then another, linking them end to end until they made two eleven-foot-long booms pointing out into space. He then unhitched himself from the footholds to float a giant sail of thermally treated gold fabric to the attachment points at the poles' ends. Next, he reeled the sail until it covered the orbital workshop like a golden duvet, shielding Skylab from the heat of the sun.

Before returning indoors, Garriott swam to the end of the windmill telescope on the other side of the spacecraft. Since Huntsville, he'd vowed to find a moment in space to put his toes on the edge of Skylab and look down.

And what he saw was, in a sense, a distance equal to the entire length of the Grand Canyon. In another sense, he saw the equivalent of a cross spider staring over a smallish asteroid, perhaps the size of the one named after the schoolteacher who died on her way to space. And in a completely different sense, the science pilot saw nothing at all.

Once back inside Skylab, Garriott discovered Arabella had spun her first web in microgravity.

The distance between a man and the moon is a spider hiking the Oregon Trail. The distance from a spider to the end of her six-inch silk tether is a man drifting on a sixty-foot umbilical. A man tumbling from end to end of a space station is a spider free-falling down a four-foot web.

For a spider is a particle and a man is a particle and the spider attracts the man with a force directly proportional to the product of their masses and inversely proportional to the square of their distances.

For a man is least distant from a spider when the world he knows is multiplied by cosmic exponents.

For a spider is most distant from a man when she no longer has the tools to refer to herself.

●● ▬ ● ▬ ●●

The first web she made was loose and haphazard, a funhouse mirror of her gridded, Earth-spun work. Since she could not feel the weight of her body on the strands, the silk she spun was of varied and impractical thickness. Few of the lines were taut or straight. The web looked like the worn-out shawl of a sideshow palmist, or a sea net from which any fish could manage escape. It is the kind of web only spun on Earth when a spider has just molted, or is quite near her death. It is not unlike a web spun by an amputee spider, or the spider that a Swiss pharmacologist spiked with d-amphetamine in 1948.

●● ▬ ● ▬ ●●

Space was a kind of stimulant for the Skylab crew, who, in the second week of their nine-week flight, radioed Mission Control for extra work. Science Pilot Garriott logged twenty-two hours in a single mission day. Though NASA had proposed sending them to space with a game console and movie projector, all the crew really wanted to do for R and R was stare out the window and monkey around in the microgravity. Because space awakens things in the human body. The men had become more dexterous and less nauseated. Zero-g decompressed their vertebrae; each man stretched at least an inch by splashdown.

In the evenings, the men floated to the ring of hulking white lockers that encircled one end of the workshop and they ran laps, running the "wheel" from wall to ceiling and back down like three Astaire hamsters. Or they would tumble and flip in their white socks and boxers, gliding into one another, making water-ballerina shapes. They challenged each other to contests of floating—from the trash airlock, down past Arabella's TV cage, past the kitchen and through the hatches, all the way to the command module that brought them to space—without flapping an appendage. "We might have had a shot at the Olympics," Garriott later quipped. The science pilot called this feat "playing Spiderman."

The lights came on in Arabella's cage, simulating sunrise. It was six days after her release from the vial and two weeks after launch, and her air was still charged with that defeating kind of nothing that kept her lines from catching and confounded her body when she tried to rappel. But the walls of the cage were solid in a way she could understand, so she connected a taut bridge line in the short gap between them. The only way to make a web in flight, she discovered, was to avoid flight—to stay grounded.

Clinging to the walls and corners of the cage, she made more short silk lines, pulled them as tightly as she could, and walked along them (rather than free-falling) to affix every radial, every spiral turn. She used the length of her hind legs to measure each spiral; each ring matched the distance between her spinneret and the tip of her back claw. The central claws of her third pair of legs clung to the silk like grappling hooks.

It was a less ambitious web in certain aspects. She had ringed it in fewer spirals, and omitted the crucial lopsidedness of lining the web-bottom with that stickier trapping silk. But the structure was even and tight. Back home, a human face crashing through it could have thought it the work of any earthbound arachnid.

From Commander Bean's journal, August 7: "Arabella finished her web perfectly. When Owen told Jack at breakfast, Jack said, 'Well, that's good. I like to see a spider do something at least once in a while.'"

Bean again, on August 8: "Arabella ate her web last night, and spun another perfect one."

Commander Bean on Aug 10: "Owen did the Spider TV three times today."

The men and their cargo were orbiting Earth every other hour, curving fifty degrees north and south of the equator—ringing the parallels, rising and sinking. Their remaining tethers to the earth were the kind that are difficult to pull on—teleprinter dispatches, the transmitted sinusoid waves of their wives' voices, the electric grid of Enid, Oklahoma, which blinked for Garriott when his hometown knew he was passing overhead. And though their distance never increased from the day they docked, the human cargo drifted further with each spacewalk, each tube of liquid spaghetti, each wrench slipping from their fingers that they no longer reflexively reached out to catch.

• • ▬ • ▬ • •

August 11 was supposedly the crew's day off, but none of the three wanted rest. Neither did Arabella, who spun another lovely web— her fourth in as many days. Garriott had taken to calling her "our friend Arabella" and noted the day before that she was "near a very large horizon at this point." In his transmission back to Earth on August 12, he described his friend moving her web from the corners of her cage to front and center—a much more telegenic place—where it stretched ever closer to the webs of home. There was a delighted lilt in his voice when he reported how, "without the benefit of previous experience and simply working on her own, she figured out a very nice solution to the problems of zero gravity."

Houston woke the men every "morning" with news updates, but the crew knew the worst events of the day were always missing. NASA had arranged for Skylab to hear of no plane crash at Logan Airport, no coup in Chile, no serial killer found fifteen miles from the very control room that shot their news into the sky. Back on Earth, Skylab was, of course, making its own headlines—at least an article a day on the men and their work hounding comets and setting records for nights slept in orbit. And most of the stories found a way to weave into their paragraphs news of the little spider in the TV-ready box.

Footage of her spinning aired on the *CBS Evening News* with Walter Cronkite. Her image, perched at the center of an impressive silver-toned web, ran in *Science News*, the *Los Angeles Times*, and along the AP wire. With each web spun, observed, photographed, and transmitted, things became stickier between Arabella, the astronauts, and the people of Earth. NASA had planned to let her die in space after a few days, but as the *Washington Post* said, Arabella had "earned the affection of the crew" so completely that, "midway through the flight, Owen Garriott asked what could be done to prolong that relationship."

Who could possibly condemn to death the weaver of the universe's first space web? A creature that journalist Lee Edson called "probably the most distinguished spider in the world"? And how could anyone be surprised when Edson announced, "NASA made another high-level decision. Arabella will be permitted to return to Earth with the astronauts on September 25."

By then, Mission Control had its own mascot spider, Arachne, living in a glass cage in the Command Center. They could look at her when they heard Garriott in space, describing his friend Arabella. They radioed an order for Garriott to set aside a housefly-sized morsel of that evening's space-dinner: filet mignon. "When Arabella is in her cage, carefully place a piece near her legs," ordered CAPCOM Richard Truly. According to the *New York Times*, "The spider loved it, and proceeded to build another web."

Each new web held the planet tighter in her grip. Only Arabella could bridge the distance between all earthbound creatures and the incomprehensible developments of Skylab—the X-ray maps of the galaxy, the Technicolor evidence of holes in the sun. As she steadied her slow steps along the straight line of her web and gripped the solid products of her body for support, she was walking back to what the people of Earth could understand: an organic narrative of success amid what on TV and in the papers must have seemed a dark and unnatural nebula. She did so naked, assisted by nothing but the tangible: her legs, her cage, the lightbulb someone turned on for her every eighteen hours. Dogged and stealthy, the spider created an earthly object in that wild and distant nothing. And alongside all the work of the floating men, her work was weighty and familiar—a lifeline tailor-made for the people of earth.

For a spider in the center of her web is less distant from you than a man backflipping through a spaceship in his underwear. For a man in space is a decorated Navy pilot in alien coveralls, unraveling a golden fleece to save his billion-dollar ship from frying in the nearby sun. For the spider in space still only knows a garden sun. She lifts the same eight unsheathed legs that tread any apple branch. She isn't an honorary Doctor of Science or a Fellow at the American Astronomical Society. She's never seen the earth while standing on its moon.

For a spider in space has no title, just the sweet name of one of our daughters. When we speak it, the name makes the sound of a bell in the air.

● ● ━ ● ━ ● ●

Commander Alan Bean retired a few years after splashdown to start a painting career, and nearly every canvas he finishes is a scene in oil of a man on the moon. After commanding a space shuttle voyage in the early 1980s, Pilot Jack Lousma ran for state senator and lost. Owen Garriott returned to space a decade after Skylab, then helped send his son to the International Space Station twenty-five years later—the first American to pass space travel down a generation.

Arabella made it back to Earth, but just barely. According to NASA, they found the spider curled into a ball in her transport vial the day after splashdown. "An autopsy will be performed," reassured Reuters. It ruled dehydration as the cause of her death, and then there was nothing else to do but catalog her with the rest of the Skylab data.

Preserved in formalin and arranged in a black cylinder with a plexiglass viewing front, she's now item A19740484001 in the National Air and Space Museum, on display with Skylab's other equipment. Among the titanium alloy, the neoprene, the epoxy-resin ablative and the resin-impregnated fiberglass honeycomb, she is the rare logged item on display that is listed as "organic matter."

Though he's outlived her by over forty years, Garriott has not forgotten the spider. In 2013, he sat on a NASA panel held for the fortieth anniversary of Skylab—a panel that also included a science pilot from the contemporary space station. When this younger scientist referenced early work with animals in microgravity, Garriott, now a vigorous eighty-two-year-old, all but interrupted him. He sat forward in his chair and pushed his words out faster than he could pronounce them. His blue eyes widened as he looked into the small crowd of reporters and students. "Does the name Arabella ring a bell with any of you?"

Behind him was a large projection of the official Skylab III embroidered mission patch, which had been sewn to the shoulders of all Skylab personnel. The circular patch is a take on Leonardo da Vinci's *Vitruvian Man*, in his notorious power stance. Behind the naked man is a circle half filled with a globe and half filled with a flaming sun. The man seems to float in the center of the patch, splitting the blue and the orange. He reaches to the edges of the frame with all eight of his appendages.

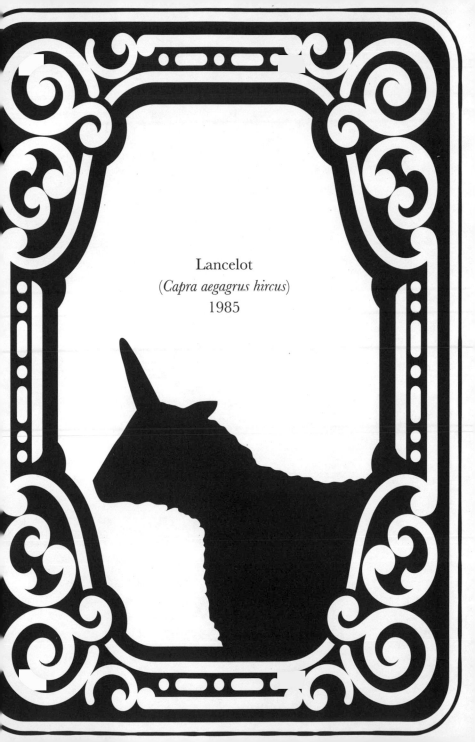

Lancelot
(*Capra aegagrus hircus*)
1985

(Children are, briefly, somewhat different.)
John Berger, "Why Look at Animals?"

WHEN I WAS IN FIRST grade, a migrating humpback whale swam seventy miles upriver from the San Francisco Bay and found itself marooned in a freshwater slough north of Rio Vista. The national papers filed dozens of stories about the whale—soon named Humphrey—and the nightly news checked in with his progress for nearly a month, with extended Humphrey segments on weekend shows like *60 Minutes*. I caught as much of it as I could from my home on the other side of the country. The video footage rarely offered much—usually just shots of the small flotillas surrounding Humphrey, or of the people, both aboard and ashore, banging cookware to frighten the whale downriver. I remember one still image of a man in a fishing boat tossing buckets of salt water onto Humphrey's back. Too lethargic to flip or spout, Humphrey was just a long, slick log floating near scores of excited humans. That was all I ever knew of him on earth.

This could be why I filed Humphrey the humpback into the same category as My Little Pony or the Easter Bunny. Nothing about the Humphrey tale was anything short of magic to me. When Peter Jennings said Humphrey's name on the news, I ran into my living room with the same enthusiasm I felt upon hearing the *Smurfs* theme.

They finally got Humphrey to swim back to open water by plunging a high-tech speaker into the river and blaring the cries of feeding humpbacks, which he followed. These cries were described to me—by the news, by my teacher—as "song," so my seven-year-old understanding was that this whale had been crooned to safety. I can still see the finale footage—how Disney-perfect it looked!—of the boats leading a shadow of a gigantic fish under the largest bridge I'd ever seen. They were all in a faraway land no one in my family had ever visited, and that whale swam home right under the most fantastic-sounding bridge: the Golden Gate.

Most of the animal world held for me this incorrect magic, which spurred me toward an impasse—an inability to note the contextual divide between the animals that shared our world and the ones that were invented to please me. At whatever moment of a child's development that she learns to separate natural wonder and wondrous tale, something inside me misfired. Only from the distance of adulthood can I even see the disconnect, and I'm not sure if this is the case with other young children of my era, because I grew up alone.

I was born at the tail end of the seventies, four days before Easter, and all the cards sent to my mother were covered in pastel chicks and lambs. The nurses wrote my sex and my hospital ID number on cards with pink dancing bears, which they stuck to the bassinet and the door of our room. Someone gave me a stuffed hare in a navy vest that sits near me in early photos. In all these shots, I am a bleary-eyed, furry little thing.

My mother took me home in a receiving blanket patterned with geese in blue bonnets. She mailed announcements of my length and weight on cards bearing crewel-stitched puddle ducks. The early facts of my life were written into a book with a fat bunny on the cover. I slept in a yellow Beatrix Potter crib set, surrounded by Peter Rabbit, Tom Kitten, and Hunca Munca Mouse.

This was the year after critic John Berger published the first version of his "Why Look at Animals?," an essay often hailed as a founding document in the field of animal studies. Berger's essay begins by outlining a loss: once, and for a very long time, animals were crucial to human life; they surrounded people and culture in a close circle that connected to both the everyday and the spiritual. But, Berger says, due to the Industrial Revolution and the ripple effects of the twentieth century, "every tradition which has previously mediated between man and nature was broken." As Berger saw it, animals were no longer the "messengers and promises" of culture, or our partners in survival. Instead, they were available only as neutered pets, as kept zoo creatures, or as "commercial diffusions of animal imagery." These commercial images, stuffed toys, and storybook animals aped "the pettiness of social practice," Berger said, adding that "the books and drawings of Beatrix Potter are an early example."

According to my Peter Rabbit baby book, the first song I could sing was "Old MacDonald," and I knew the word "kitty" by the end of my first year. For my birthday, Mom baked a chocolate cake in the shape of a cat with uncooked spaghetti in the icing (for whiskers). By then, I'd tell any interested party what the kitty said, what the doggie said, even what the fishy said. In my crib at night, I watched a mobile of padded quadrupeds spin to "Farmer in the Dell." My green bikini top was shaped into a pair of googly-eyed frogs, I wore a brown-checked dress covered in bespectacled owls to meet Santa Claus, and I was given for Easter a stuffed rabbit in a pink pinafore—my best friend, Tammy—that I rarely let go of through kindergarten.

I realize now that, growing up in a house shared only with two working adults, I was a fairly lonely girl, which left inside me a tender spot—not broken, just bruised—that I can still locate. When pressed, the lonely spot feels like being lost; it reminds me that, for years, I was the only member of my species (the species of modern kid). It's a wonder this didn't convince me that Humphrey, the only creature of his kind for miles, was a part of my real world. But the tender spot was most certainly soothed by the promises and messages of (what I thought were) animals. I obsessed over creature books, toys, and movies. *The Poky Little Puppy* taught me to read. *Charlotte's Web* taught me that rats were gross and that my mother would die one day. *Koko's Kitten* taught me that every creature just wants something soft to care about. I still can quote the majority of these animal stories from memory; they kept me company.

At night, after I cleaned my room by cramming all its loose contents in the hamper at the foot of my bed, I could hear my stuffed animals inside the box, whimpering in the dark. Alone in the yard, I often pretended I was an orphan in the wilderness. I'd splash around in the rain and find reasons to fall in the mud. I fantasized what kind of animal would find me and take me (perhaps literally) under its wing. Sometimes it was a natural animal, like a wild horse or a wolf, but just as often it was something more magical—a luck dragon or a white horse that could fly. They were all the same to me, of course.

The year of Humphrey, I turned seven and celebrated at a pizza parlor known for its "live" animatronic critter band. In the dining area, the robot animals performed at programmed intervals—a brown bear on drums, a gorilla on keyboards, a polar bear on guitar. A curtain drew around them at the pauses. I snuck behind it and looked up the pleated skirt of the tambourine player—a giant, deactivated cheerleader mouse. Her purple robot eyelids had frozen, half-raised, when she lost power.

•• ■• ■• ••

The sharpest moment in "Why Look at Animals?" involves a glance between a beast and an earlier human. Berger is vague about where and when this might have taken place, but his man and animal, as they stare at one another, experience a deep understanding. They recognize both their mutual power and their separated secrets. Berger calls their connection an "unspeaking companionship" grounded in the lack of a common tongue. It allows human and animal to live along "parallel lines," during which the human feels the animal's gaze enhancing "the loneliness of man as a species."

Berger says "the look between animal and man . . . may have played a crucial role in the development of human society." We were inspired by their proximity—both what we knew of them and what we didn't. And while the product of this isolating gaze gave animals a spiritual power and a place in human art, their nearness as both livestock and predator kept them "real" and vital. "They were subjected *and* worshipped, bred *and* sacrificed," Berger says. Thanks to that Bergerian gaze, animals covered the major components of human life—both religious and quotidian, both biological and mythic. Because of that look, a lion could become for humans both a threatening neighbor and a god. That look assured that animals "belonged *there* and *here*."

But according to Berger, this gaze is something I would never myself experience, because the real animals had been extracted from my own *here* long before I arrived. I wholeheartedly recognize this. *Here* for me was but a synthetic wilderness. *Here* was Minnie

Mouse jamshorts and Thundercats bathtub toys, plush mammals I could take to bed and tell my secrets to. But, still, my *here* was never without an animal representation. More than people and more than machines, false animals inhabited my field of vision (even though they could never return my gaze). It is important for me to remember that these animals were, essentially, fact-less. But because they were omnipresent and because they outnumbered everything else, this was the universe—an absolute onslaught of fake animal presence was every fiber of my *here*. I wonder if Berger ever took into account what might happen to future generations when those "commercial diffusions" of animal shapes became available to young minds at such a fever pitch.

In his essay, the affected twentieth-century humans are non-descript capitalists, but it seems we should take them all as fully formed. In Berger's thinking, little space exists for children. The bereft "now" of his essay is full of adults who stand within a generation of the earlier human-animal connection. But what happens when a person is born after the mess we were in circa "Why Look at Animals?" What happens when she begins not just forming herself, but *finding* herself among a sham menagerie?

I'd argue that my animal imaginings essentially were spiritual, and that they made an intense *there* for me via the thousands of hours of cartoons and books, the *Wonderful World of Disney*, and my own goofy solo play. It certainly wasn't the *there* on which entire cultures were built (was it?), but I believed it like a zealot. Despite the fact there were no real ones around me, I used these warped ideas of animals to help me solve problems, I sang animal songs to soothe myself, and I certainly spoke to them in a kind of prayer.

My faith—and I was reared far from religion—was this blank space in which the late twentieth century "animals of the mind" were free to romp as I saw fit. I now have a spiritual *there*, and it is my only one, warped as it may be, where Berger says nothing exists anymore. My sense of story, art, imagining, the words for writing, the ways of coping—they all come from the experiences that my phony zoo contributed to my early youth.

My mom took me to the National Zoo in DC, where a thousand other onlookers and I watched a giraffe give birth ("Can you believe we were *here* when it happened?"). At the Bronx Zoo, I rode a camel. My dad put me on his shoulders at a low-rent South Carolina zoo and I poked at an ostrich with a stick until it bit my Keds sneaker. At Zoo Atlanta's week-long summer camp, I watched *Wild World of Disney* videos in the lab behind the reptile building, where one of the yellow snakes had the same name as me. We were gently led through parts of the flamingo enclosure and we even played red rover in the empty polar bear exhibit. Running and yelling where the polar bears roamed each morning felt like touring a celebrity home.

Most of these zoos had undergone renovations into our current breed of animal tourism, their verdant habitats and outdoor viewing pavilions replacing the concrete cages and tire swings of earlier times. These zoo designs were no longer the meager "theatre props" Berger decried in the late seventies, with only "dead branches of a tree for monkeys, artificial rocks for bears, pebbles and shallow water for crocodiles." This is not to say, of course, that they were any more natural.

According to Berger, "The zoo cannot but disappoint." It only presents "lethargic and dull" specimens removed not only from their natural environments, but also from any natural drive or individual interest. They cannot inspire, or even exchange that crucial glance with the humans who visit them. There are no "parallel lines" between human and animal life in a zoo, because, as is the case with house pets, the animal life has become so dependent on humans that it is no longer viable alone.

But I do not recall a disappointment like Berger describes, because at the zoos, I was often too busy to look at any animal for very long. Here is something else Berger was probably unable to foresee: my visits in the 1980s were to zoos that had marginalized the marginalized animals. Along with creating more convincing habitats, these new zoos built scores of distracting "discovery kiosks" and activities—rock walls, coloring stations, kiddie trains—that lined the paths from one enclosure to the next. At dozens of sidewalk carts, you could buy T-shirts or concentrated orange juice in a plastic container—*shaped like an actual orange!* It was more like visiting a theme park than a menagerie.

No longer was the main purpose to see, as Berger says, the "originals" of the stuffed mammals from our bedrooms. I was there to gallop about and play, to be my own animal. The kiddie games ran interference for the zoo creatures which, for me, were more like the robot critter band at that pizza place. They were an underscore to a party, the jazzy accompaniment to an afternoon outside with horseplay, a picnic, and maybe a present or two.

Where Berger says every zoo-goer raised on Peter Rabbit asks herself, "Why are these animals less than I believed?" a decade later, I think I'd have been more likely to ask, "Why are these animals even *here*?"

The section on zoos is the grand finale of the essay; Berger concludes with the lamentable image of a crowd at an animal cage, standing before a creature that will not look at them in any meaningful way. The crowd, then, can only look at each other as "a species which has at last been isolated." Here he says, is the failure of zoos. Perhaps this explains why, by the time I arrived at one, they'd given me other things to do. And, it must be said, several things to buy. Maybe this is the real question kids of my era should have asked when they skipped into the zoo: "Since commerce took real animals from me, shouldn't it have to make for me a viable replacement?"

●● ▬ ● ▬ ●●

That same year as the Humphrey story and the zoo camp, my grandparents took me to the Ringling Brothers and Barnum & Bailey Circus. This was their year of Lancelot—"the Living Unicorn," as he was billed on the 1985 souvenir program. I bought the program with three dollars of my own money and, after the circus, thumbed through it for weeks until the glossy pages fell to pieces. It said the Living Unicorn had just wandered into the big top one day the previous year, provenance unknown. Lancelot was ageless; there were no facts to weigh him down other than the fact that, according to the program, he ate rose petals for dinner. In the full-color photographs, he usually stood next to a spangly, Miss-America-cute woman, his long white hair—not so much a mane as a suit of poodle curls—gleaming and very possibly permed.

The horn at the top of his head was prodigious: twice as thick as that of the title character in *The Last Unicorn*. It was also covered in opalescent pink paint, trunking up from Lancelot's forehead in a glittery shaft. In one photograph, he appeared with two children about my age. The blond boy in the photo smiled out toward the photographer, but the little girl next to Lancelot stared right at the unicorn with unabashed awe, like she'd forgotten all about the person taking her picture. Lancelot himself gazed into the middle distance, looking like a little, white Rick James. Who knows what he was thinking.

The program also featured a pullout poster that I taped to my closet door. It was a Lisa Frank–style portrait of Lancelot in a hot pink frame, above the caption "I Saw the Living Unicorn!" I'm not certain how many differences I noticed, back then, between the illustrated poster unicorn and the photographed one. But now, it's obvious that the drawn unicorn is horsier, with a straight-up mane, a fuller muzzle and a longer, broader neck. The eyes are much less hircine, and they stare straight into the viewer.

At the circus, Lancelot didn't gallop in; he rode. His entrance was on a hydraulic float trimmed in Grecian curlicues, with a curved dais at the top of it, slathered in gold paint. On the dais was a waving handler, dressed sort of like Glinda the Good Witch, who stood beside Lancelot. The unicorn himself had a tiny gold pedestal atop the dais, on which he could only arrange his front two feet.

A follow spot stuck to the vehicle as it zoomed around the ring; Lancelot stood erect, but sort of jostled in the motion of the float. Schmaltzy orchestral music boomed from the Civic Center speakers. From my seat, Lancelot was little more than a white furry blob. But when his shellacked horn, firm and proud on his cranium, caught the spotlight, everyone around me inhaled. He was much smaller than a horse—maybe pony-sized—which, being small myself, I found exciting.

I now wonder why the circus didn't just strap a horn to an actual pony. They could have easily used showbiz magic to sell that trick from an arena-sized distance. But the circus was working a different angle with this critter that, even from yards away, was no horned horse. Perhaps they needed a horn that would look more legitimately rooted in photo close-ups. They knew I would obsess over that program, so they wanted a unicorn that read biologically true at home, away from the smoke and spotlight. But I think it's more likely that they wanted to surprise us over anything else, even if that surprise involved a ridiculous specimen. It's brilliant circus logic: that this jarring, not-horse-body was so weird, it would make sense when you learned it subsisted on flower petals. In other words, the circus hoped the more unnatural Lancelot looked, the happier I'd be.

What I recall feeling at that matinee is an aching deep in that tender, only-child place inside myself. It softened the suspect details of Lancelot's freaky body. Under the "tent," I had a foundational understanding something was fishy about that unicorn, but still, I ached for him. The emotion, for me, wasn't about his realness; it was about sitting (relatively) near something that represented offsite magic. This is a reverse of Berger's zoo animals—failed attempts at real versions of stuffed bedroom toys. Lancelot was the glorious opposite: a fake spectacle at the center of the ring that confirmed all my homespun, isolated imaginings to indeed be believable magic. Wild and insane Lancelot was before me; he could be both visited *and* dreamed about. The unicorn goat was, for me, both *there* and *here*.

Along with sensing, and then ignoring, that the unicorn was phony, I also knew it was probably some kind of victim, though even that didn't deter my pleasure. I could not yet grasp how costly a real animal's presence in my imagination could be. Of this I am the most ashamed, because I know a version of that ignorance still lives in me. I didn't grasp, or I refused to consider, what kind of subjection was possible—the various ways humans open up and alter other creatures.

The tales of Beatrix Potter never mention that billy goats are born with their horn-buds loose, floating right under the skin for the first week of their lives. It never occurred to me that a person might vivisect a newborn goat—graft the buds from their rightful place above the eyes to the frontal bones of the skull. Ten more days into the baby goat's life, this process would be impossible, as by then the skull has ossified. But an enterprising human with a fresh goat on her hands can divide the kidskin forehead into four dermal flaps and rearrange them—in a process called "pedicling"—so that when the horns form, they fuse over the pineal gland and erupt as a single keratin pillar.

How could I ever have imagined that, even as obsessed with fantasy as I was? Where in my wildest seven-year-old dreams was US Patent #4,429,685, which legally awards authorship of "a method for growing unicorns" to a separatist religious leader turned veterinary surgeon named Timothy G. Zell, alias Otter G'Zell, alias Oberon Ravenheart?

After a New York City performance, someone called the ASPCA about Lancelot. The FDA performed a careful examination and declared him a perfectly healthy, if deformed, goat. Another phone call was made to the New York Consumer Protection Board to challenge whether Lancelot could legally be billed "unicorn." The circus responded with a full-page ad in the *Times*—"Don't Let the Grinches Steal the Fantasy!"—and refused to admit that it bought Lancelot from Zell for a six-figure sum. Lancelot lasted another national tour, and then disappeared from the circus, who hasn't mentioned him since.

Of course, none of this controversy was in my head when I saw Lancelot. I was just one of the thousands of Americans born in 1978 that watched a surgically altered goat ride a golden chariot around their local civic center. But here I am, thirty years later, trying to explain what happens when I look at animals, and the creature that palpitates my tenderest spot is that hot mess of an animal—over the humpback whale, the baby giraffe, or the snake with my own name.

Maybe this is the coda to the final zoo scene of "Why Look at Animals?," as this is what an animal consciousness can now become. Four decades past Berger, the animal of *my* mind is a gaudy but satisfying creature that had little to do with fact from the get-go. Though unprecedented and unnatural, his form still exists. It holds a wonky, mythic nature—which is the only nature a kid like me will ever understand.

The animal of my mind is bright and dandy and painfully incorrect. He's living proof of my whacked-out desires and my ability to ignore cruel realties. And weirdly enough, he's government-sanctioned; Lancelot follows the rules. The lines between our two lives are not so much parallel as bent—by sheer will, like spoons—until they touch.

Rather than a wild mustang or a trusty hound or even a Beatrix Potter bunny, my relationship with animals best resembles this cream-rinsed, mutant goat with a watery eye—this survivor of backwoods surgery with a pastel-bedazzled wang sprouting from his brain. The *here* and *there* of Lancelot grow together in my place, in the parts of my mind that—at the site of my beginning—were pulled back and rotated to sprout an outrageously new thing. There's a distinct possibility that every time I write about an animal, I am only writing about him—which might also mean, horrifyingly, that I'm only writing about myself.

Yes, Lancelot says, and turns to me with his sparkling, goaty eyes. He looks right into my lonely soul and something in my cranium shakes. *Come see what has been made for you—see the Living Unicorn. Come here, Elena Marie. Look into my eyes. Can you even believe all the ways you and I were made for each other?*

Koko
(*Gorilla gorilla gorilla*)
1988

Ms. Patterson finally scolded her and signed "bad gorilla," whereupon
Koko signed "funny gorilla" and laughed.

Associated Press

KOKO THE GORILLA TELLS A FAMOUS JOKE: Father-gorilla, Mother-gorilla, Baby-gorilla hungry. Need work.

Mustache-man tell: "What work?"

Father-gorilla tell: "Really together show. Fine show. Good practice. Lights-off good."

Mustache-man tell: "Hurry, give me."

Father-gorilla tell: "'Hello!' do Mother-gorilla; 'Hello!' do Father-gorilla. Together dance; clap people. Father-gorilla harmonica; Mother-gorilla clowntime; clap people. 'Hello!' do Baby-gorilla. Skateboard do, puppet dance do; clap people. Father-gorilla kiss, Mother-gorilla kiss; gorilla hug, Mother-gorilla nipple find; clap people. Nipple kiss, nipple rub, nipple pinch, nipple slap, nipple-on-bottom, nail clipper nipple, many many nipple touch. Tongue nipple. Nipple sandwich."

Mustache-man tell: "Who nipple?"

Father-gorilla tell: "ALL nipple. Now Father-gorilla, Mother-gorilla peekaboo pickle. Poke stomach. Peekaboo pickle with pat-bottom. With walk-up-my-bottom. Pull-out hair. Nasty time. Mean love. Mother-gorilla leash-on pickle; skateboard ride do. Clap people.

"Mother-gorilla find Baby-gorilla. Little noodle pull. Zip mouth shut. Strangle tadpole. Mayonnaise necklace. Father-gorilla there; sit Father-gorilla. Thirsty Father-gorilla lick; Mother-gorilla strap-on. Baby-gorilla sit Mother-gorilla. ALL PEEKABOO PICKLE. Trouble pickle.

"Baby-gorilla get Ingrid. 'Hello!' do Ingrid. Ingrid turn-around; Baby-gorilla wrestle. Ingrid trouble. Devil Ingrid. 'You bad dirty toilet Ingrid.' Ingrid pudding do. Ingrid laugh; Ingrid eat. Ingrid sick. Mother-gorilla taste. Bottle-match! Ingrid electric pudding. Ingrid get Father-gorilla. Pickle bottle-match! Peekaboo pickle on fire now!

"Ingrid hole smoke-ring blow. Mother-gorilla hole blow harmonica. Father-gorilla dance, balloon-on-noodle. Baby-gorilla clowntime, balloon-on-tadpole. Ingrid hole smoke-smoke. Around together skateboard do—smoke noodle balloon harmonica ride all! Harmonica hole play 'Purple Rain!' All MAYONNAISE RAIN! All finished! Thank you."

Mustache-man tell: "Wow. What name show?"

Father-gorilla tell: "WE WONDERFUL SNOB PEOPLE!"

Mustache-man smile-frown.

Drapes.

Osama
(*Crocodylus niloticus*)
1998

We do not easily distinguish, emotionally, between a human eating an animal and an animal eating a human.

Alistair Graham, *Eyelids of Morning*

*O*SAMA THE CROCODILE LIVED ON the banks of Lake Victoria in Uganda.

So begins "A Crocodile Called Osama," a passage from the *Conquering Comprehension* student workbook. Written for Australian early readers, *Conquering Comprehension* is divided into twenty-six units, each unit consisting of a brief essay that models a mode of writing, followed by a half dozen critical questions. Unit two, "Literary Description," is a detailed scene of a girl named Abigail looking out a window. Unit four, "Procedure," is a bullet-pointed kayaking how-to. And the five paragraphs of "A Crocodile Called Osama" make up the entirety of unit three, "Factual Description."

> *He was nearly five metres long, weighed a tonne and, during his long life of sixty years, had killed and eaten eighty-three people from the village of Luganga on the shores of the lake.*

The simple fuchsia sketch of a Nile crocodile that hogs much of unit three's page space offers very little that's either factual or descriptive. The drawn reptile has a narrower body than a sexagenarian croc would. The illustration's eyes are not googly enough. The belly should be thicker and dirty purple; the tail should be longer and striped. And lots of apex predator facts go undescribed in the text: how Osama could hold his breath under water for an hour, or halt his digestive juices to postpone hunger for one year. How he could walk on land if need be, and how, in his younger days, he might've galloped. How he hovered in the brack of his lake for up to a week in pursuit of a single creature—one ton of stillness in ambush.

> *Apart from the deeds of his horrifying past,*
> *Osama had developed a new and fiendish habit:*

These are the facts of size and biology that conquered centuries of human comprehension. These facts led people to name Nile crocodiles as their gods—greedy deities who rob and swindle and fuck on the backs of half-eaten humans. They drove men, these facts, to adorn a tame croc with jewels and to sing to it at festivals, and they inspired humans to decorate themselves as crocs, or feed the entrails of their dead kings to the monsters in their lakes. These facts make fishermen smear the hulls of their boats with crocodile fat to deflect lightning, or cover their skin with croc brains to ward off further croc attack.

> *he had begun tipping over the villagers' fishing*
> *boats to grab a fisherman and even jumped into*
> *the boats themselves to claim his victims.*

But none of these facts of nature, legend, or hunger appear in unit three, "Factual Description." All the 320 words of the passage offer its young readers is the "description" of a conquering and the "fact" of an incomprehensible name.

> *The village people called in Officials of the Uganda Wildlife Authority who devised a clever plan to catch the man-eater.*

When *Conquering Comprehension* was first published in 2006, Osama, though sixty, hadn't been named Osama for long. The first decade of his bloody run, people had called the crocodile John Major. Before that, he was called *goonya, mamba,* or *temsah,* depending on who was pointing at him from the relative safety of the shore. And further back in time, when Herodotus described him as a floating pair of eyes and a spine in the water, he was named "pebble worm" or "pebble dick" or, most alarmingly, "pebble man."

> *They draped the lungs of a dead cow, a tasty morsel, over the branch of a tree near Osama's lair, and waited a whole week for the crocodile to strike.*

It isn't difficult to see a name as a kind of factual description. Naming halts kinetic energy, as do the arresting properties of fact. Names sink an unconquerable entity—a hurricane, a rogue virus, a man-eater—with the weight of a fresh, human-made label. And a naming is also a proving—of how we cannot abide the unknown power of natural caprice when it feeds on us. We doubt our ability to get inside the brain of an erratic and inhuman thing-of-the-world, like a monster storm or an epidemic. We cannot wear its ideas as our own in an effort to best it. So we name it, in hopes of yanking it from the chaos-machine in which it naturally thrives.

*And strike he did, leaping out of the water and
seizing the bait in his mighty jaws.*

We work together as a like-minded group to rename the thing-
of-the-world. And in this way, we convince ourselves that we've
gained a modicum of control. This makes an act of naming de-
fensive and it forces whatever has jammed our processors into a
tighter, more comprehendible space. Perhaps, we think, this will be
enough to keep us afloat when that unconquerable, newly named
thing approaches us—when it bucks the natural facts of the world
on which we float.

It was a fatal mistake.

In 1998, when the croc then known as John Major began jumping into the little boats, a new fact spread along the shore: that
this beast was too terrible to even belong to nature. A rumor also
spread that any surviving fishermen—those still intact season after
season—were not alive because of wiliness or simple luck. Some
spirit had to be looking out for the un-man-eaten men, whispering
to them from under their boats out on the lake. They must be in
Faustian cahoots with an unearthly evil, the other fishermen now
understood. And in understanding this, they renamed the croc for
the devil himself. A few along that stretch of Lake Victoria will still
insist the croc's true name is Satan.

*Concealed within the lungs was a copper snare
attached to a long rope.*

And then, in August 1998, bombings in two nearby embassies
killed two hundred people and wounded twenty times that. The
name of the man behind the bombings became a new fact for the

people to bite. This new moniker was a better name than Satan, even, with its extra syllable and its sonic distance from "saint." By the time the crocodile had taken ten more victims, the new and explosive human name sat square on the beast's scuted back. It was past Satan, this name of the human stranger who could neither be caught nor comprehended. For nothing could be wilder, nothing more fearsome, than a man who eats men with a big bomb. Osama. The closest you can be to be a devil and still carry the facts of a man.

> *The more Osama struggled, the more he became entangled.*

Giving a human's name to a man-eater is a noteworthy and questionable practice. We aren't always compelled to do so—see the Beast of Gévaudan, the Leopard of Rudraprayag, the Malawi Terror-Beast. See *Jaws*. It means something to name a predator not after a region, a synecdoche, or a pebble dick, but with a little first name, just as you would a human baby. Why would we want to bring a skilled man-eater so close to the way we call ourselves?

> *Fifty men pulled on the rope attached to the snare and slowly dragged the furious, struggling crocodile out of the water.*

Did we do this because we wanted to plant inside the croc a humanesque scheming? Do we need to give the croc the power to conjure the evil ideas of which our human devils are capable? It could be that it's just too difficult to truly *hate* a crocodile, with its flat eyes, cold blood, and heart shaped like a peanut. After it has taken so many, we must find a way to feel the hatred reserved for those of our kind who eat our kin.

Soon the villagers had Osama bound, gagged and at their mercy.

Or perhaps it's just that nothing is more incomprehensible than a beast capable of blood *sport.* We comprehend the animal that strikes human attackers, or strikes to protect its cubs. A poisonous bite or slash to the thorax is the understandable, ham-fisted work of nature, and Lord knows we humans have done little to inspire the rest of the kingdom's trust. But the unconquerable man-eaters' attacks are not in retaliation, and thus humans, to them, are probably still nothing more than lumps of digestible parts. Though it hurts us to admit it, the components that make us invent, travel, or even blow up crowded embassies are still no more difficult to swallow than the legs of a wildebeest or the heart of a stupid gazelle.

Imagine their surprise when they were told by the Wildlife Authority that they were not allowed to finish him off.

The man's name that was given to this beast actually holds another man-eater at its roots. In Arabic, the name Osama means "feline predator" or "lion" or "mark of the lion." It is one of dozens of Arabic first names with leonine associations, and there are similar men's names in Yiddish, French, Gaelic, Hebrew, Turkish, Vietnamese. So many of us fancy naming our human babies—especially male ones—after lions, perhaps because it brands them with grace and force. Osama-as-lion is the name of a tawny king and his mighty heart. Osama-as-lion is a powerful man, relaxed in his status, and perhaps self-assured enough to see order in his own incomprehensible hunger.

Even Osama, it seemed, had his rights.

"Lion" is also what we called the two man-eaters that stalked railroad workers in 1898, as the men built the tracks that connect the Indian Ocean to Osama's very lake. An exact century before the man-Osama bombed the embassies and the croc-Osama was rechristened, two unnamed lions dragged 135 railroad men from their flimsy lakeside tents—nearly one per night. The foreman would awake each morning to find "the ground all round covered with blood and morsels of flesh and bones." The bald-faced lions—the beasts had no manes—would lick the skin off their victims immediately, so rampant was their taste for fresh human blood.

In the end, the villagers took their revenge in another way:

The foreman finally shot them, of course, and the remaining men went back to the railroad. When the crew finished building, the foreman took the lions' skins as rugs for his study, where he wrote *The Man-Eaters of Tsavo*—an international bestseller. He later bequeathed the lion skins to a museum in Chicago. And there the man-eaters stay, renamed FMNH 239-69 and FMNH 239-70.

Osama was to spend the rest of his days in a concrete enclosure at a crocodile farm, becoming the father of little crocodiles who would be made into crocodile handbags and shoes.

We are now beyond predation; that is the myth of humans. It's a lonely understanding, if you think on it: the easiest predator to know is the predator within us, and the only creatures we give the right to devour us are creatures just like ourselves. No tiger hiding in the darkness, no white whale. Only an embassy bomber with a soft skull, no claws, and dull teeth, although he is named after a lion.

His diet would be limited to dead chickens.

Or only another soft human, this one named after a day of feasting, born in the 1920s at the top of Osama's lake. When the crocodile was about thirty, this man had renamed himself His Excellency, President for Life, Field Marshal Al Hadji Doctor, Idi Amin Dada, Lord of All the Beasts of the Earth and Fishes of the Seas. When he dumped thousands of his countrymen into Lake Victoria, a rumor circulated among the people that he was feeding the lake's crocodiles and perhaps heightening their taste for human meat. But others spread an alternate rumor—still held by some as fact—that *he* had taken to eating the men when it suited him to do so. When pressed about this scandalous detail, he looked away with his famous protruding eyes and said, "I don't like human flesh. It's too salty for me."

It was an inglorious end for the mighty beast, al-
though many would argue that he got off lightly.

Four years after this man fled from his palace to a comfortable exile in Libya, a crocodile from Lake Victoria began making a name for himself.

WORD AND PHRASE MEANING
*What other words fit into the word family that
contains horrifying and fiendish?
terrifying   fearsome   modest   fearful
ghastly   gentle   kindly   grisly
frightening   shocking   horrific   repugnant
appalling   horrendous naughty

Which brings us back to "A Crocodile Called Osama," the revenge text for Aussie eleven-year-olds that focuses more on the facts of a name than the facts of any beast. Young readers pass over the name Osama eight times in three hundred words, incanted like a hex, paired with a litany of angry verbs. They read the name as it is "bound," "gagged," "struggling," and "at the mercy" of its captors. They see the name begrudgingly afforded "rights," then forced into a concrete cell for eternity.

READING BETWEEN THE LINES—Inferential Meaning

What do you think of the plan to catch Osama? (That is, was it clever, well thought out, requiring patience?)

What surprised the villagers when Osama was captured?

Do you think they should've been surprised?

What do you think should have been done with Osama? Do you think he "got off lightly"?

Why do you think that?

The book's target market are children that live seven thousand miles away from the crocodile when they read about him. At the end of the passage, the critical follow-up questions don't so much test what they understand about crocodiles, but rather what they know of a human's wishful thinking. Perhaps such wishful thoughts are the most predatory facts of all.

What does gagged mean?

There is no record of the death of the crocodile called Osama. His human counterpart was conquered in 2011, and it's doubtful the croc lasted those six years as brood stock. By the time these two Osamas were no longer facts of the earth, Osama the ten-foot-tall Asiatic elephant had trampled over a dozen men and women in Assam, and Osama the lion had eaten at least fifty unsuspecting Tanzanians.

MORE ACTION

Find Lake Victoria in Uganda, using your atlas.
Find out about "Sweetheart," a large and terrifying crocodile that lived in the Northern Territory of Australia.

In 2001, twin jaguar cubs were born at a Bolivian animal center, and one was nicknamed Osama "because he was the bad one of the two." Though cranky and uncontrollable, he never killed anyone; he never even made it out of the animal center, but his twin brother did. That cub, once it reached adulthood, became famous for stalking and devouring a handler at the Denver Zoo in 2007. Back in Bolivia, his first handlers had named that killer twin jaguar after George W. Bush.

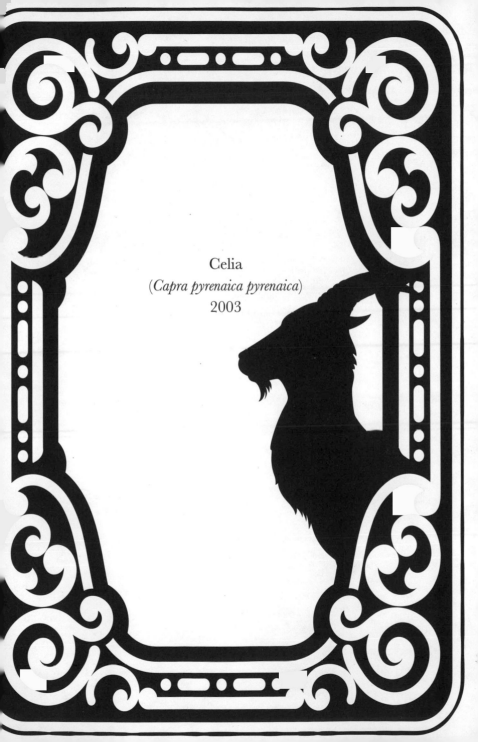

Celia
(*Capra pyrenaica pyrenaica*)
2003

SIR: There is a need for a word in taxonomy, and in medical, genealogical, scientific, biological, and other literature, that does not occur in the English or any other language. We need a word to designate the last person, animal, or other species in his/her/its lineage.

Letter to the editor of *Nature*, April 1996

THE LAST WOOLLY MAMMOTHS DIED on an island now called Wrangel, which broke from the mainland twelve thousand years ago. They inhabited it for at least eight millennia, slowly inbreeding themselves into extinction. Even as humans developed their civilizations, the mammoths remained, isolated but relatively safe. While the Akkadian king conquered Mesopotamia and the first settlements began at Troy, the final mammoth was still here on Earth, wandering an Arctic island alone.

The last female aurochs died of old age in the Jaktorów Forest in 1627. When the final male perished the year before, its horn was hollowed, capped in gold, and used as a hunting bugle by the king of Poland.

The last pair of great auks had hidden themselves on a huge rock in the northern Atlantic. In 1844, a trio of Icelandic bounty hunters found them in a crag, incubating an egg. Two of the hunters strangled the adults to get to the egg, and the third accidentally crushed its shell under his boot.

Martha, the last known passenger pigeon, was pushing thirty when she died. She'd suffered a stroke a few years earlier, and visitors to her cage at the Cincinnati Zoo complained the bird never moved. It must have been strange for the older patrons to see her there on display like some exotic, since fifty years before, there were enough of her kind to eclipse the Ohio sun when they migrated past.

Incas, the final Carolina parakeet, died in the same Cincinnati cage that Martha did, four years after her. Because his long-term mate, Lady Jane, had died the year before, it was said the species fell extinct thanks to Incas's broken heart.

When Booming Ben, the last heath hen, died on Martha's Vineyard, they said he'd spent his last days crying out for a female that never came to him. The *Vineyard Gazette* dedicated an entire issue to his memory: "There is no survivor, there is no future, there is no life to be recreated in this form again. We are looking upon the uttermost finality which can be written, glimpsing the darkness which will not know another ray of light."

Benjamin, the last thylacine—or Tasmanian tiger—perished in a cold snap in 1936. His handlers at the Beaumaris Zoo had forgotten to let him inside for the night and the striped marsupial froze to death.

The gastric brooding frog—which incubates eggs in its belly and then vomits its offspring into existence—was both discovered and declared extinct within the twelve years that actor Roger Moore played James Bond.

Turgi, the last Polynesian tree snail, died in a London zoo in 1996. According to the *Los Angeles Times*, "It moved at a rate of less than two feet a year, so it took a while for curators . . . to be sure it had stopped moving forever."

The same year, two administrators of a Georgia convalescent center wrote the editor of the journal *Nature*, soliciting a name for an organism that marks the last of its kind. Among the suggestions were "terminarch," "ender," "relict," "yatim," and "lastline," but the new word that stuck was "endling." Of all the proposed names, it is the most diminutive (like "duckling" or "fingerling") and perhaps the most storied (like "End Times"). The little sound of it jingles like a newborn rattle, which makes it doubly sad.

While *Nature*'s readers were debating vocabulary, a research team in Spain was counting bucardos. A huge mountain ibex, the bucardo was once abundant in the Pyrenees. The eleventh Count of Foix wrote that more of his peasants wore bucardo hides than they did woven cloth; one winter, the count saw five hundred bucardos running down the frozen outcrops near his castle. The bucardo grew shyer over the centuries—which made trophy hunters adore it—and soon disappeared into the treacherous slopes for which it was so well designed.

Though a naturalist declared it hunted from existence at the turn of the twentieth century, a few dozen were spotted deep in the Ordesa Valley in the 1980s. Scientists set cage traps, which caught hundreds of smaller, nonendangered chamois. It was frustrating work, and bucardo numbers dwindled further as the humans searched on. By 1989, they'd trapped only one male and three females. In 1991, the male died and eight years later, the taxon's endling, Celia, walked right into the researchers' trap.

She was twelve when they shot her with a blow dart and tied white rags over her eyes to keep her calm. They fit her with a tracking collar and a pulse monitor and biopsied two sections of skin: at the left ear and the flank. Then Celia was released back into the wild to live out the rest of her days. Of the next ten months we know nothing; science cannot report what life was like for Earth's final bucardo. But the *Capra pyrenaica* before her had, probably since the late Pleistocene, moved through the seasons in sex-sorted packs. In the female groups, a *bucarda* of Celia's age would serve as leader. When they grazed in vulnerable spaces, she'd herd her sisters up the tricky mountain shelves at the first sign of danger, up and up until the group stood on cliffs that were practically vertical. Celia, however, climbed to protect only herself that final winter—and for at least three winters before that, if not for most winters in her rocky life.

It is dangerous to assume that an endling is conscious of its singular status. Wondering if she felt guilty, or felt the universe owed her something—that isn't just silly; it's harmful. As is imagining a bucardo standing alone on a vertical cliff, suppressing thoughts of suicide. As is assuming her thoughts turned to whatever the mountain ungulate's version of prayer might be. Or hoping that, in her life, she felt a fearlessness impossible for those of us that must care for others.

The safe thought is that Celia lived the life she'd been given without any sense of finality. She climbed high up Monte Perdido to graze alone each summer, and hobbled down into the valley by herself before the winters grew too frigid. She ate and groomed and slept, walked deep into the woods, and endured her useless estrus just as she was programmed to do—nothing further.

But then again, a worker ant forever isolated from its colony will walk ceaselessly, refusing to digest food, and a starling will suffer cell death when it has no fellow creature to keep it company. A dying cross spider builds a nest for her offspring even though she'll never meet them, and a pea aphid will explode itself in the face of a predator, saving its kin. An English-speaking gray parrot once considered his life enough to ask what color he was, and a gorilla used his hands to tell humans the story of how he became an orphan. Not to mention the countless jellyfish that, while floating in the warm seas, have looked to the heavens for guidance.

Though problematic, it's still easy to call these things representative of what unifies our kingdom: we are all hardwired to live for the future. Breeding, dancing, nesting, the night watch—it's all in service to what comes later. On a cellular level, we seem programmed to work for a future which doesn't concern us *exactly*, but that rather involves something that resembles us. We all walk through the woods, our bodies rushing at the atomic level toward the idea that something is *next*. But is there space in a creature's DNA to consider the prospect of *no* next? That one day, nothing that's us—beyond ourselves—will exist, despite the world that still spins all around us?

Six days into the new millennium, Celia's collar transmitted the "mortality" beep. A natural death—crushed by a falling tree limb, her neck broken and one horn snapped like a twig. In a photo taken by the humans that fetched her, she seems to have been nestled on her haunches, asleep. They sent Celia to a local taxidermist and then turned to the cells they'd biopsied. After a year spent swimming in liquid nitrogen at 321 degrees below zero, the cells were primed to divide. The *Los Angeles Times* ran a long article about what might happen next, quoting an environmentalist who warned, "We don't have the necessary humility in science."

At the lab, technicians matched a skin cell from Celia with a domestic goat's egg cell. The goat-egg's nucleus was removed, and Celia's nucleus put in its place. Nearly all the DNA of any cell lives inside its nucleus, so this transfer was like putting a perfect Celia curio into the frame of a barnyard goat.

After a mammal's egg cell is enucleated, it is common for nothing to happen. But sometimes, the reconstructed cell reprograms itself. Thanks to a magic humans don't totally grasp, the nucleus decides it is now an egg nucleus and then replicates not as skin, but as pluripotent, able to split into skin cells, blood cells, bone cells, muscle cells, nerve cells, cells of the lung.

While this DNA technology evolved, the Celia team cultivated an odd harem of hybrid surrogates—domestic goats mated with the last female bucardos. They had hybrid wombs that the scientists prayed would accept the reconstructed and dividing eggs. In 2003, they placed 154 cloned embryos—Celia in a goat eggshell—into 44 hybrids. Seven of the hybrids were successfully impregnated, and of those seven, just one animal carried a zygote to term. The kid was born July 30, 2003, to a trio of mothers: hybrid womb, goat egg, and magical bucardo nucleus. Genetically speaking, however, the creature was entirely *Capra pyrenaica*. And so, thirteen hundred days after the tree fell on Celia, her taxon was no longer extinct—for about seven minutes.

The necropsy photos of the bucardo kid are strangely similar to those of Yuka, the juvenile mammoth found frozen in permafrost with wool still clinging to her body. Wet, strangely cute, and lying stretched out on her side, the newborn looks somehow timeless. Her legs seem strong and kinetic, as if she were ready to jump up and run. All of her systems were apparently functional, save her tiny lungs.

In her hybrid mother's womb, the clone's lung cells mistakenly built an awful extra lobe, which lodged in her brand-new throat. The kid was born struggling for air and soon died of self-strangulation. Lungs seem the trickiest parts to clone from a mammal; they're what killed Dolly the sheep as well. How fitting that the most difficult nature to re-create in a lab is the breath of life.

The term we now use for the procedure of un-ending an endling has been around for decades, though it was rarely used. "De-extinction" first appeared in a 1979 fantasy novel, after a future-world magician conjures domestic cats back from obscurity. But when the Celia team reported their findings to the journal *Theriogenology*, they didn't use the word. A few scientific papers in fields ranging from cosmology to paleobiology check the name, but it was left almost entirely to science fiction until a dozen years postbucardo. A MacArthur Fellow chided the term's clunkiness, calling it "painful to write down, much less to say out loud." But eventually, the buzzword stuck.

"De-extinction" made its popular debut in 2013, in a *National Geographic* article. To celebrate the coming-out of the term—and the new ways it would allow humans to mark animal lives—the magazine held a conference at their headquarters with lectures organized into four categories: Who, How, Why/Why Not, and Wild Again. Among the How speakers was Ordesa National Wildlife Park's wildlife director, who recounted the Celia saga. The four-syllable term tangled with the director's Castilian accent, but people still applauded when he called Celia's kid "the first ez-tinc-de-tion." As the audience clapped, the director bowed his head, obviously nervous. Behind him was a projected image of the cloned baby, fresh from her hybrid mother and gagging in the director's latexed hands. The clone's tongue lolled out the side of her mouth.

Earlier that morning, an Australian paleontologist confessed his lifelong obsession with thylacines, despite being born nine years after the Tasmanian tiger's demise. "We killed these things," he said to the audience. "We shot every one that we saw. We slaughtered them. I think we have a moral obligation to see what we can do about it." He then explained how he'd detected DNA fragments in the teeth of museum specimens. He vowed to first find the technology to extract the genetic code from the thylacine tooth-scraps, then to rebuild the fragments to make an intact nucleus, and finally to find a viable host womb where a Tasmanian tiger's egg could incubate—in a Tasmanian devil, perhaps.

The man's research group, called the Lazarus Project, had just announced their successful cloning of gastric brooding frog cells. The fact that the cells only divided for a few days and then died would not deter his enthusiasm. "Watch this space," he said. "I think we're gonna have this frog hopping glad to be alive in the world again."

Later in the conference, a young researcher from Santa Cruz outlined a plan that allowed humans to "get to witness the passenger pigeon rediscover itself." But after de-extinction, he said, the birds would still need flying lessons. So why not train homing pigeons to fly passenger routes? To convince the passenger babies they were following their own kind, the young scientist suggested coating the homers with blue and scarlet cosmetic dyes.

That afternoon, the chair of the Megafauna Foundation mentioned how medieval tales and even the thirty-thousand-year-old paintings in Chauvet Cave would help prepare Europe for the herds of aurochs he hoped to resurrect. The head of the conference's steering committee sounded almost wistful when he concluded at the end of his speech, "Some species that we killed off totally, we could consider bringing back to a world that misses them." And a Harvard geneticist hinted that mouse DNA could be jiggered to keep the incisors growing from the jawline until they protruded, tusklike, from the mouth. This DNA patchworking could help fill a gap in our spotty rebuild of the mammoth genome, he said.

Shortly after that talk, a rare naysayer—a conservation biologist from Rutgers—addressed the group: "At this very moment, brave conservationists are risking their lives to protect dwindling groups of existing African elephants from heavily armed poachers, and here we are in this safe auditorium, talking about bringing back the woolly mammoth; think about it."

But what exactly is there to think about? What can *thinking* do for us, really, at a moment like this one? We're knee-deep in the Holocene die-off, slogging through neologisms that remind us what is left. These speeches—of extravagant plans, of Herculean pipe dreams, and of *missing*—are more than thought; they admit to a spot on our own genome. Perhaps we've always held, with submicroscopic scruples, the fact of this as our *next*. The first time a forged tool sliced a beast up the back was the core of this lonely cell, and then that cell set to split, and now each scientist—onstage and dreaming—is a solitary cry of this atomic, thoughtless fate.

To dispatch animals, then to miss them. To forget their power and use our own cockeyed brawn to rebuild something unreal from the scraps. Each speech, at this very moment, is a little aria of human understanding, but it's the kind of knowledge that rests on its haunches in places far beyond thought.

And at that very moment, the last Rabbs' fringe-limbed tree frog was dodging his keepers at a biosecure lab in Atlanta. Nicknamed Toughie, the endling hadn't made a noise in over seven years.

And at that very moment, old Nola and Angalifu, two of the six remaining northern white rhinos, stood in the dirt of the Safari Park at the San Diego Zoo with less than twenty-four months to live. Their keepers had already taken Angalifu's sperm and would do the same for Nola's eggs, housing the samples in a lab that had already cataloged cells from ten thousand species. It was a growing trend—this new kind of ark, menagerie, or book of beasts—and it carried a new term for itself: the "frozen zoo."

The planet's other northern whites, horns shaved down for their own protection, roamed Kenya's Ol Pejeta Conservancy under constant armed watch. And Celia's famous cells were buzzing in their cryogenic state, far from Monte Perdido, still waiting for whatever might come next.

And at that very moment, way up in northwest Siberia, a forward-thinking Russian was clearing a space to save the world. As the permafrost melted, he said, it would eventually release catastrophic amounts of surface carbon into the atmosphere. To keep the harmful gases in the rock-hard earth, the Russian and his team wanted to turn the tundra back into the mammoth steppe: restoring grassland and reintroducing ancient megafauna that would stomp the dirt, tend the grass, and let the winter snows seep lower to cool the deep land. The reintroduced beasts, he swore, would send the tundra back in time.

He proposed that for every square kilometer of land there be "five bison, eight horses, and fifteen reindeer," all of which had already been transported to his "Pleistocene Park." Here was a space where earlier versions of all these beasts had lived in the tens of thousands of years prior. Eventually, once the science caught up, he would bring one elephant-mammoth hybrid per square kilometer, too.

And so here is a picture of next: some model of gargantuan truck following the Kolyma River—rolling over the open land where mammoths once ran for hundreds of miles. Like a growing many of us, the Russian sees the moment in which that truck's cargo door opens and a creature—not quite Yuka but certainly not elephant—lumbers out into the grass. Her first steps would be less than five hundred miles as the crow flies, out and out over the Arctic, from the island where the last living mammoth fell into the earth 3,600 years ago.

The Russian's process—making new beasts to tread on the bones of what are not quite their ancestors—has a fresh label for itself, as everything about this world is new. The sound of this just-coined word, when thrown by a human voice into a safe auditorium, carries with it the hope of a do-over, and the thrust of natural danger.

That new word is *re-wilding*.

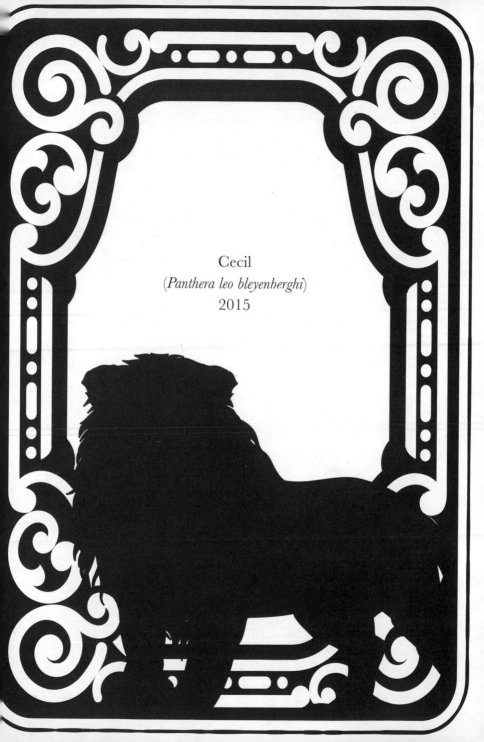

Cecil
(*Panthera leo bleyenberghi*)
2015

ASSOCIATED PRESS: YOU'VE EXPRESSED SOME regret over the way this transpired. Is your regret about taking this lion or being kind of caught up in this whole swirl?

Dr. Walter Palmer: I made an initial statement on that and I'm going to stay true to that, OK? Obviously, if I'd have known this lion had a name and was that important to the country, or a study, obviously, I wouldn't have taken it.

Minneapolis Star Tribune: Do you know, I'll take a stab at this . . .

Dr. Walter Palmer: Nobody in our party knew, before or after, the name of this lion.

COLLECT THEM ALL!

Notes

"Jeoffry" began when I learned that the most famous cat poem in English is actually a fragment. Apparently, Christopher Smart's *Jubilate Agno*—written from a madhouse in the mid-eighteenth century—has several lost sections, and it is believed that the "My Cat Jeoffry" section is missing its left-hand side. I did my best to mimic intact portions of the *Jubilate* when I "finished" the poem (aka the "Let" lines). All the "For" lines on the right are Smart's.

The text of "Koko" comes entirely from the thousand-plus-word vocabulary of a famous sign language-using gorilla. I've not strayed from that documented lexicon, and I've tried to evoke the syntactical pairs that myriad sources report the gorilla employing, but the actual telling of the joke is my invention (though Koko *is* known for her sense of humor).

Bibliography

SHARED SOURCES

Barber, Richard. *Bestiary*. Rochester, NY: Boydell & Brewer, 1992.

Barnes, Jonathan. *The Complete Works of Aristotle: the Revised Oxford Translation*. Princeton, NJ: Princeton University Press, 1984.

Berger, John. "Why Look at Animals?" *About Looking*. New York: Vintage, 1992.

Chaline, Eric. *Fifty Animals That Changed the Course of History*. Richmond, Ontario: Firefly Books, 2015.

Cummins, John. *The Hound and the Hawk: The Art of Medieval Hunting*. New York: St. Martin's, 1988.

Curley, Michael J., trans. *Physiologus*. Chicago: University of Chicago Press, 2009.

Kaloff, Linda. *Looking at Animals in Human History*. London: Reaktion Books, 2007.

Pliny the Elder. *Natural History*. Translated by Harris Rackham. Cambridge: Harvard University Press, 1938.

YUKA

Barcroft TV. "Lion Attacks Elephant: Brutal Kill Caught on Camera." YouTube video, 01:22. Posted January 20, 2014. https://www.youtube.com/watch?v=vp9EC4tS-Q0.

Blaszczak-Boxe, Agata. "Woolly Mammoth Mummy Yields
    Well-Preserved Brain." *Live Science*, November 7, 2014.
    http://www.livescience.com/48625-mummy-woolly
    -mammoth-brain-revealed.html.

Cave of Forgotten Dreams. Directed by Werner Herzog. Orland Park,
    IL: MPI Home Video, 2011. DVD.

Cohen, Tamara. "The Amazing Ginger Mammoth." *Daily Mail*,
    April 4, 2012. http://www.dailymail.co.uk/sciencetech
    /article-2124991/Siberian-mammoth-Yuka-Ice-Age
    -creatur-perfectly-preserved-10-000-years.html.

Guthrie, R. Dale. *Frozen Fauna of the Mammoth Steppe*. Chicago:
    University of Chicago Press, 1990.

Guthrie, R. Dale. *The Nature of Paleolithic Art*. Chicago: University
    of Chicago Press, 2005.

Human Planet. "Stealing Meat From Lions." Discovery Channel
    Online video, 02:25. http://www.discovery.com/tv-shows
    /human-planet/videos/stealing-meat-from-lions/.

Larmer, Brook. "Of Mammoths and Men." *National Geographic*,
    April 2003. Accessed June 22, 2016. http://ngm.nationalgeo
    graphic.com/2013/04/125-mammoth-tusks/larmer-text/.

Rudaya, Natalia, Svetlana Trofimova, Plotnikov Valerii
    Valerievich, and Snezhana Zhilich. "Landscapes of the
    'Yuka' Mammoth Habitat: A Palaeobotanical Approach."
    Review of Palaeobotany and Palynology 14 (March 2015): 1-8.

"Meet Yuka, Siberia's Latest Star With Strawberry Blonde Hair, Discovered in the Ice By Tusk Hunters." *Siberian Times,* April 7, 2012. Accessed June 22, 2016. http://siberiantimes.com /science/casestudy/news/meet-yuka-siberias-latest-star-with -strawberry-blonde-hair-discovered-in-the-ice-by-tusk-hunters/.

Thurman, Judith. "First Impressions." *New Yorker,* June 23, 2008.

Trinkaus, Erik, and Jiří Svoboda. *Early Modern Human Evolution in Central Europe: the People of Dolní Věstonice and Pavlov.* Oxford: Oxford University Press, 2006.

Walker, Tim. "Woolly Mammoth: Secrets from the Ice." *BBC Nature,* April 5, 2012. http://www.bbc.co.uk/nature/17525074.

THE WOLF OF GUBBIO

Badke, David. "Wolf." *The Medieval Bestiary: Animals in the Middle Ages.* January 15, 2011. http://bestiary.ca/beasts/beast180.htm.

"St. Francis of Assisi." *Catholic Encyclopedia Online.* http://www.catholic.org/encyclopedia/view.php?id=4829.

Trevisa, John. *On the Properties of Things: John Trevisa's Translation of Bartholomaeus Anglicus De Proprietatibus Rerum.* Oxford: Clarendon Press, 1988.

House, Adrian and Karen Armstrong. *Francis of Assisi: A Revolutionary Life.* Mahwah, NJ: Paulist Press, 2003.

Lopez, Barry. *Of Wolves and Men.* New York: Scribner, 2004.

Murray, Wendy. *A Mended and Broken Heart: the Life and Love of Francis of Assisi.* New York: Basic Books, 2008.

Okey, Thomas, trans. *The Little Flowers of Saint Francis.* Mineola, NY: Dover, 2003.

GANDA

Bartrum, Giulua. *Albrecht Dürer and His Legacy.* Princeton: Princeton University Press, 2003.

Bremer-David, Charissa. "Animal Lovers Are Informed." In *Oudry's Painted Menagerie: Portraits of Exotic Animals in Eighteenth-Century Art,* edited by Mary Morton, 91-104. Los Angeles: Getty Museum, 2007.

"Number 75: Dürer's 'Rhinoceros'." *A History of the World in 100 Objects.* BBC Online, 2010. http://www.bbc.co.uk/ahistory oftheworld/about/transcripts/episode75/.

Bubenik, Andrea. *Reframing Albrecht Dürer: The Appropriation of Art 1528-1700.* Surrey, UK: Ashgate, 2013.

Clarke, T.H. *The Rhinoceros from Dürer to Stubbs, 1515-1799.* London: Philip Wilson Publishers, 1988.

British Pathé. "Dalí Paints Rhino 1955." YouTube video, 00:39. Posted April 13, 2014. https://www.youtube.com/ watch?v=lyPtU8WZD3M.

Dalí, Salvador. *Dalí on Modern Art: The Cuckolds of Antiquated Modern Art.* Translated by Haakon M. Chevalier. Mineola, NY: Dover, 1996.

Dalí, Salvador. *Diary of a Genius*. New York: Doubleday, 1965.

Eisler, Colin. *Dürer's Animals*. Washington, DC: Smithsonian, 2001.

Enright, Kelly. *Rhinoceros*. London: Reaktion Books, 2008.

Gibson, Ian. *The Shameful Life of Salvador Dalí*. New York: Norton, 1998.

Masterpieces of the British Museum: Dürer's Rhinoceros. London: Quantum Leap Video, 2007. DVD.

Latham, Robert, trans. *The Travels of Marco Polo*. New York: Penguin, 1958.

Prinz, Jesse. "Dürer's *Rhinoceros*: Art, Exotica, and Empire." *Artboullion*, January 3, 2015. http://www.artbouillon.com/2015/01/durers-rhinoceros-art-exotica-and-empire.html.

Quammen, David. *The Boilerplate Rhino: Nature in the Eye of the Beholder*. New York: Scribner, 2000.

Ridley, Glynis. *Clara's Grand Tour: Travels with a Rhinoceros in Eighteenth-Century Europe*. New York: Grove, 2004.

Russell, Francis. *The World of Dürer*. New York: Time Life Education, 1967.

Salley, Victoria. *Nature's Artist: Plants and Animals by Albrecht Dürer*. New York: Prestel Verlag, 2003.

Spinks, Jennifer. *Monstrous Births and Visual Culture in Sixteenth-Century Germany.* New York: Routledge, 2009.

Strauss, Walter, ed. *The Complete Engravings, Etchings, and Dry Points of Albrecht Dürer.* New York: Dover 1972.

SACKERSON

Adams, Joseph Quincy. *A History of English Theaters from the Beginning to the Restoration.* New York: Houghton Mifflin, 1917.

"Anecdotes of Bear Baiting." *The Gentleman's Magazine* 103 (June 1833): 486.

Baldwin, Elizabeth. "But Where Do They Get the Bears?: Animal Entertainments in Sixteenth- and Seventeenth-Century Cheshire." Paper presented at the SITM Colloquim, Groningen, Netherlands, July 2-7, 2001.

Chambers, Robert. "Bear Baiting." *The Book of Days, Volume 2.* Philadelphia: Lipincott, 1899.

Fudge, Erica. *Perceiving Animals: Humans and Beasts in Early Modern Culture.* Chicago: University of Illinois Press, 2002.

Hoffle, Andreas. "Sackerson the Bear." *REAL: Yearbook of Research in English and American Literature.* Edited by Herbert Grabes, 161-175. Gottinger, Germany: Hubert & Company, 2001.

Mabillard, Amanda. "Entertainment in Elizabethan England." *Shakespeare Online,* August 20, 2000. Accessed June 21, 2016. http://www.shakespeare-online.com/faq/entertainment.html.

Morris, Sylvia. "Exit, Pursued By a Bear? Bear-baiting in Shakespeare's London." *The Shakespeare Blog.* January 13, 2013. http://theshakespeareblog.com/2013/01/bears/.

Nott, J. Fortune. "Bears." *Wild Animals, Photographed and Described.* London: Crown, 1886.

Walford, Edward, ed. "London Theatres." *The Antiquary* 12 (July 1885): 44-48.

Wheatley, H.B. *London Past and Present.* London: Scribner, 1891.

JEOFFRY
Curry, Neil. *Christopher Smart.* Devon: Northcote House, 2005.

Hawes, Clement, email interview with the author, May 13, 2014.

Mounsey, Chris: *Christopher Smart: Clown of God.* Lewisburg: Bucknell University Press, 2001.

Smart, Christopher. "For I Will Consider My Cat Jeoffry." *The Penguin Book of English Verse.* Edited by PJ Keegan. London: Penguin, 2004.

---. *The Poetical Works of Christopher Smart, I: Jubilate Agno.* Edited by Karina Williamson. Oxford: Clarendon, 1980.

VOGEL STAAR
Ashoori, Aidin and Joeseph Jankovic. "Mozart's Movements and Behaviour: A Case of Tourette's Syndrome? *Journal of Neurology and* Neurosurgery 78, no. 11 (November 2007): 1171-1175.

Chaiken, Marthalea, Jorg Bohener, and Peter Marler. "Song
Acquisition in European Starlings, *Sturnus vulgaris*." *Animal
Behaviour* 46, no. 6 (December 1993): 1079-1090.

Deutch, Otto Eric. *Mozart: A Documentary Biography.* Redwood City,
CA: Stanford University Press, 1966.

Feare, Christopher. *The Starling.* Oxford: Oxford University Press,
1984.

Gutman, Robert W. *Mozart: A Cultural Biography.* New York:
Harcourt Brace, 1999.

Harer, Ingeborg. "Musical Venues in Vienna, Seventeenth
Century to Present." *Performance Practice Review* 8 (Spring
1995): 83-92.

Karhausen, Lucien. *The Bleeding of Mozart: A Medical Glance into
His Life, Illness, and Personality.* Bloomington, IN: Xlibris, 2011.

Keim, Brandon. "Starling Flocks Behave Like Flying Magnets."
Wired, March 13, 2012. www.wired.com/2011/11
/starling-flock/.

---. "The Startling Science of a Starling Murmuration." *Wired*,
November 11, 2011. www.wired.com/2012/03/starling-
flock-dynamics/.

Robbins Landon, H.C., ed. *The Mozart Companion: A Guide to
Mozart's Life and Music.* New York: Schirmer, 1990.

Marler, Peter and Hans Slabbekoorn. *Nature's Music: The Science of Birdsong*. Oxford, UK: Elsevier, 2004.

Rothenberg, David. "Why You Can't Teach a Starling to Sing." National Wildlife Federation online, April 1, 2006. https://www.nwf.org/News-and-Magazines/National-Wildlife/Birds/Archives/2006/Why-You-Cant-Teach-a-Starling-to-Sing.aspx.

Ross, Alex. "The Storm of Style." *Listen to This*. New York: Farrar, Straus and Giroux, 2010.

Spaethling, Robert. *Mozart's Letters, Mozart's Life*. New York: Norton, 2000.

Stafford, William. *Mozart's Death: A Collective Survey of the Legends*. London: Macmillan, 1991.

Stap, Don. *Birdsong: A Natural History*. New York: Scribner, 2005.

ThePIPdesign. "Starling song over five minutes straight." Youtube video, 05:55. Posted April 20, 2014. https://www.youtube.com/watch?v=Y2pjUlp2Cy0.

Tyson, Alan. *Mozart: Studies of the Autograph Scores*. Cambridge, MA: Harvard University Press, 1990.

Wakin, Daniel J. "After Mozart's Death, an Endless Coda." *New York Times*, August 24, 2010.

West, Meredith J., and Andrew King. "Mozart's Starling." *American Scientist* 78 (March-April 1990): 106-114.

Wright, Craig. *Listening to Music*. 7th Ed. Boston: Cengage 2013.

HARRIET

Australia Zoo. "Harriet: Our Famous and Much-Loved Giant
Galápagos Tortoise." https://www.australiazoo.com.au
/our-animals/harriet/.

Benchley, Peter. "Galápagos: Paradise in Peril." *National Geographic*,
April 1999.

"Brisbane Flood of 1893 Left Most of Metropolis in Ruins."
Sydney Daily Mirror, May 31, 1985.

Chambers, Robert. *A Sheltered Life: The Unexpected History of the
Giant Tortoise*. Oxford: Oxford University Press, 2006.

Darwin, Charles. *Autobiographies*. New York: Penguin, 2006.

---. *The Voyage of the Beagle*. New York: Penguin, 1989.

Darwin, Francis, ed. *The Life and Letters of Charles Darwin*. Project
Gutenberg, 2013. http://www.gutenberg.org/files/2087
/2087-h/2087-h.htm.

Fleay, David. *Living With Animals*. Melbourne: Lansdowne
Press, 1960.

Stewart, Robin. *Darwin's Tortoise*. Melbourne: Black Publishing
2005.

Townsend, Charles Haskins. *The Galápagos Tortoises and Their Rela-
tion to the Whaling Industry: A Study of Old Logbooks*. New York:
New York Zoological Society, 1925.

White, Gilbert. *Portrait of a Tortoise: Extracted from the Books and Letters of Gilbert White.* London: Chatto and Windus, 1946.

Williams, Brian. "Harriet's 92 Million Minutes of Fame." *Brisbane Courier Mail,* October 10, 2005.

Young, Peter. *Tortoise.* London: Reaktion Books, 2003.

WAR PIGS
American Battle Monuments Commission. *77th Division: Summary of Operations in the World War.* Washington: US Government Printing Office, 1944.

Blechman, Andrew. *Pigeons: The Fascinating Saga of the World's Most Revered and Reviled Bird.* New York: Grove, 2007.

"Coos and Kudos to Greet 'Anti-red' Pigeon Who Flew Message Through the Iron Curtain." *New York Times,* August 1, 1954.

Cummings, Richard. *Cold War Radio: The Dangerous History of American Broadcasting in Europe.* London: McFarland, 2009.

---. *Radio Free Europe's "Crusade for Freedom."* London: McFarland, 2011.

Dash, Mike. "Closing the Pigeon Gap." *Smithsonian* online, April 17, 2012. http://www.smithsonianmag.com/history/closing -the-pigeon-gap-68103438/.

Ferrell, Robert. *Five Days in October: The Lost Battalion of World War I.* Columbia, MO: University of Missouri Press, 2005.

Fisher, John. *Airlift 1870: The Balloon and Pigeon Post in the Siege of Paris.* London: M. Parrish, 1965.

Hayhurst, Jay. *The Pigeon Post into Paris 1870-1871.* Middlesex, UK: Ashford Press, 1970.

"Heroine Pigeon Now a 'Citizen'." *New York Times,* August 23, 1954.

Horne, Alistair. *The Fall of Paris: The Siege and the Commune 1870-71.* New York: Penguin, 2007.

"Iron Curtain Bird Here on Crusade." *New York Times,* August 2, 1954.

Johnson, Thomas, and Fletcher Pratt. *The Lost Batallion.* New York: Bobbs-Merrill, 2000.

Lawrence, Ashley. "A Message Brought to Paris by Pigeon Post in 1870-71." http://www.microscopy-uk.org.uk/mag /artoct10/al-pigeonpost.html.

National Archives. "Pigeon Message from Capt. Whittlesey to the Commanding Officer of the 308th Infantry." https://catalog .archives.gov/id/595541.

Navrozov, Andrei. "Popping Balloons." *Chronicles,* September 3, 2014. https://www.chroniclesmagazine.org/popping-balloons/.

Stevens, Lucy. "Siege of Paris: Pigeon Post and Balloon Mail." Paris Pigeon Post. Last modified April 26, 2011. https://parispigeonpost.wordpress.com/2011/04/06 /siege-of-paris-pigeon-post-and-balloon-mail/.

Syria Homs. "Syria - Homs - Bab Sbaa - 20120211 - People
of Baba Amr homing pigeons to send messages." Youtube
video, 05:17. Posted May 2, 2012. https://www.youtube
.com/watch?v=DNLtBgmnvv8.

"Syrians Send Messages via Carrier Pigeons in Homs." *London
Telegraph*, February 14, 2012.

Vanderbilt, Tom. "A Wing and a Prayer." *Cabinet* 11 (June 2003).

Weiss, Robert. *Enemy North, South, East, West: a Recollection of the
"Lost Battalion" at Mortain, France*. Portland, OR: Strawberry
Hill Press, 1998.

JUMBO II

Adams, Edward Dean. *Niagara Power: History of the Niagara Falls
Power Company, 1886-1918*. New York: Bartlett, 1927.

Allwood, John. *The Great Exhibitions*. London: Studio Vista, 1977.

Barry, Richard. *Snapshots on the Midway*. Buffalo: R.A. Reid, 1901.

Circus Historical Society. "*Billboard* Excerpts 1901-1903." Last
modified December 2011. http://www.circushistory.org
/History/Billboard1901.htm.

Brandon, Craig. *The Electric Chair: An Unnatural American History*.
London: McFarland, 1988.

Chambers, Paul. *Jumbo*. Hanover, NH: Steerforth Press, 2008.

Conklin, George, and Harvey Woods Root. *The Ways of the Circus:*

Being the Memories and Adventures of George Conklin, Lion Tamer.
New York: Harper, 1921.

"Coroners' Inquests: Death of the Elephant Hannibal." *New York Times,* June 2, 1865.

Daly, Michael. *Topsy.* New York: Atlantic Monthly Press, 2013.

Davis, Edwin F. Electrocution Chair. US Patent 587,649, filed January 6, 1897 and issued August 3, 1897.

Doing the Pan. "This Day in 1901 Archives." http://panam1901 .org/sitemap.htm.

Dunlap, Orrin E. "Inauguration of the Niagara-Buffalo Power Transmission." *Electrical Engineer* 22 (November 25, 1896): 540-542.

"Electricity for Executing Criminals." *Scientific American* 52 (February 14, 1885): 101.

Essig, Mark. *Edison and the Electric Chair: A Story of Light and Death.* London: Walker Books, 2005.

Friedel, Robert and Paul Israel. *Edison's Electric Light: The Art of Invention.* Baltimore: Johns Hopkins University Press, 2010.

"A Furious Elephant." *Sacramento Daily Union,* March 26, 1896.

Goldman, Mark. *High Hopes: The Rise and Decline of Buffalo, NY.* Albany: SUNY Press, 1983.

Goodwin, G.G. "The First Living Elephant in America." *Journal of Mammology* 6, no. 4 (November 1925): 256-263.

"'Gypsy' to Fight Spain." *Chicago Tribune,* January 1, 1897.

"How Much Current to Kill an Elephant?" *Scientific American* 60 (January 10, 1889): 18.

Jonnes, Jill. *Empires of Light: Edison, Tesla, Westinghouse and the Race to Electrify the World.* New York: Random House, 2004.

"Jumbo II, Enormous Elephant at Bostock's." *American Journal of Education* (August 29, 1901): 147.

"Killing Cattle by Electricity." *Scientific American* 48 (March 24, 1883): 184.

"A Man Killed by the Elephant Hannibal." *Sacramento Union*, October 28, 1862.

Marvin, Carolyn. *When Old Technologies Were New: Thinking about Electric Communication in the Late Nineteenth Century.* Oxford: Oxford University Press, 1988.

McNichol, Tom. *AC/DC: The Savage Tale of the First Standards War.* Hoboken, NJ: Wiley and Sons, 2006.

Moran, Richard. *The Executioner's Current."* New York: Knopf, 2002.

"National Archives to Display King of Siam Letter to US President." National Archives press release, September 23, 1999.

Ogden, Tom. *Two Hundred Years of the American Circus.* New York: Facts on File, 1993.

"Pan-American Exposition of 1901." SUNY Buffalo. http://library.buffalo.edu/pan-am.

Rauchway, Eric. *Murdering McKinley: The Making of Theodore Roosevelt's America.* New York: Hill and Wang, 2003.

Ray City History. "Bloody History of Gypsy the Elephant." March 7, 2012. https://raycityhistory.wordpress.com/2012/03/07/bloody-history-of-gypsy-the-elephant/.

Rydell, Robert W. *All the World's a Fair: Visions of Empire at American International Expositions, 1876-1916.* Chicago: University of Chicago Press, 1984.

Tobias, Richard. *Behemoth: The History of the Elephant in America.* New York: Harper Perennial, 2013.

"Twin Elephants Born." *New York Times,* June 25, 1903.

"Two Thousand Two Hundred Volts Fail to Kill Jumbo at Buffalo Exposition." *San Francisco Call,* November 10, 1901.

"Ugly Elephant Kills a Keeper." *Chicago Tribune,* April 26, 1901.

Wittman, Matthew. "Mandarin and the Strangling of Circus Elephants." February 17, 2014. http://www.matthewwittmann.com/strangling-circus-elephants/.

Wood, Amy Louis. "Killing the Elephant: Murderous Beasts and the Thrill of Retribution." *Journal of the Gilded Age and Progressive Era* 11, no. 3 (July 2012): 405-444.

FOUR HORSEMEN

"2012 Rolex Kentucky CCI****- Helmet Cam Analysis." Youtube video, 19:20. Posted May 2, 2012. https://www.youtube.com/watch?v=7_ETEVzzcbc.

"Berlin's Wonderful Horse." *New York Times,* September 4, 1904.

"Clever Hans Again: Expert Commission Decides that the Horse Actually Reasons." *The London Standard,* September 13, 1904.

Gothamist. "Carriage Horse Being Restrained After Crash." Vimeo video, 00:23. Posted August 16, 2012. https://vimeo.com/47686143.

McFawn, Monica. Skype interview with author. January 18, 2016.

Mister Ed: the Complete Series. Directed by Arthur Lubin. 1961-1966. Shout Factory, 2014. DVD.

Newman, Andy. "Three Are Injured When Horse Sheds Coach in Manhattan." *New York Times*, August 16, 2012.

Payne, Doug. "From Scratch to 4* Eventer in 18 mins." Youtube video, 18:50. Posted July 2, 2012. https://www.youtube.com/watch?v=njj39Wpl28I.

Pfungst, Oskar. *The Horse of Mr. Von Osten: A Contribution to Experimental Animal and Human Psychology.* Translated by Carl L. Rahn. Project Gutenberg, 2010. http://www.gutenberg.org/files/33936/33936-h/33936-h.htm

Pilliner, Sarah, and Samantha Elmhurst. *The Horse in Motion.* Hoboken, NJ: Wiley-Blackwell, 2002.

Reeve, Christopher. *Still Me.* New York: Random House, 1998.

Strahan, Tracie. "Spooked Horse 'Oreo' Recovering After Columbus Circle Accident." NBC 4 New York, August 17, 2012. http://www.nbcnewyork.com/news/local/Oreo-Spooked-Carriage-Horse-Recovering-Columbus-Circle-Accident-166593036.html.

A Wild Equus. "Clever Hans the Wonder Horse." May 27, 2012. https://wildequus.org/2012/05/27/hans-the-wonder-horse/.

Williams, Wendy. *The Horse.* New York: Scientific American/Farrar, Straus and Giroux, 2015.

Yee, Vivian. "Draft Horse that Bolted May End Up on Easy Street." *New York Times,* August 17. 2012.

Young, Alan. *Mister Ed and Me.* New York: St. Martin's, 1994.

MIKE

"All in the Neck," *Time,* October 29, 1945.

"Beheaded Chicken Calmly Lives On." *Salt Lake Tribune,* September 19, 1945.

"The Chicken that Lived Eighteen Months Without a Head."
BBC News Magazine, September 10, 2015. http://www.bbc
.com/news/magazine-34198390.

Crew, Bec. "Meet Miracle Mike, the Chicken Who Lived for 18
Months Without His Head." *Scientific American* (blog),
September 26 2014. http://blogs.scientificamerican.com
/running-ponies/meet-miracle-mike-the-chicken-who
-lived-for-18-months-without-his-head/.

"Headless Rooster," *Life*, October 22, 1945.

Katzman, Rebecca. "Here's Why a Chicken Can Live Without
Its Head." *Modern Farmer*, August 11, 2014. http://modern
farmer.com/2014/08/heres-chicken-can-live-without-head/.

Lloyd, John, and John Mitchinson. *The Book of General Ignorance*.
3rd Ed. London: Faber and Faber, 2010.

The Natural History of the Chicken. Directed by Mark Lewis. PBS
Video, 2001. DVD.

ARABELLA
Beccaloni, Jan, and Trudy Brannan. *Arachnids*. Oakland, CA:
University of California Press, 2009.

Burgess, Colin, and Chris Dubbs. *Animals in Space from Research
Rockets to the Space Shuttle*. New York: Springer, 2007.

Edson, Lee. "Skylab: No News Is Very Good News." *New York
Times*, September 9, 1973.

Hitt, David, Owen Garriott, and Joe Kerwin. *Homesteading Space: The Skylab Story.* Lincoln, NE: Bison Books, 2011.

NASA. "40th Anniversary of Skylab." Youtube video, 55:08. May 13, 2013. https://www.youtube.com/watch?v=39BjPo KaSH4.

"One Spider, Several Minnows Home from Skylab." *Washington Post,* September 25, 1973.

Portree, David, and Robert C. Trevino. *Walking to Olympus: an EVA Chronology.* Washington, DC: NASA History Office, 1987.

"Space Spiders Eat Well." *Bangor News,* August 10, 1973.

Smithsonian. "Spider, 'Arabella,' Skylab 3." https://airandspace .si.edu/collections/artifact.cfm?object=nasm_A19740484001

---. "Spider Cage, Experiment ED52, Skylab 3." https://airand space.si.edu/collections/artifact.cfm?object=nasm_ A19740484001.

"Space Spider Dies, Astros Remain Fit." *Lodi News-Sentinel,* September 17, 1973.

Summerlin, Lee B., ed. *Skylab, Classroom in Space.* Langley, VA: NASA Science and Technical Information Office, 1977.

---. *Skylab, Our First Space Station.* Langley, VA: NASA Science and Technical Information Office, 1977.

"Tests by Skylab Spiders Hint Man's Adaptability." *New York Times*, September 30, 1973.

When We Left Earth: The NASA Missions. Discovery Channel Video, 2008. DVD.

Wilford, John Noble. "Two Skylab Astronauts Set Records for Space 'Walks.'" *New York Times*, August 10, 1973.

---. "Astronauts Settle Down to Routine Jobs." *New York Times*, August 8, 1973.

Witt, Peter, Mabel B. Scarborough and Rubenia Daniels. "Spider Web-Building in Outer Space: Evaluation of Records from the Skylab Experiment." *Journal of Arachnology* 4 (1977): 115-124.

Zschokke, Samuel. "Early Stages of Orb Web Construction in *Araneus diadematus*." *Revue Suisse de Zoologie* (August 1996): 709-720.

Zschokke, Samuel, and Kensuke Nakata. "Vertical Asymmetries in Orb Webs." *Biological Journal of the Linnean Society* 144, no. 3 (March 2015): 659-672.

LANCELOT
"'Humphrey the Whale' News Reports" Filmed October 1985. YouTube video. Posted January 2009. https://www.youtube.com/watch?v=UPfgIVAzoBo.

Paddock, Richard. "Hundreds Cheer Whale: Wrong Way Humphrey Finally Returns to Ocean." *Los Angeles Times*, November 8, 1985.

Pike, Rayner. "Unicorn Verdict: It's a Goat." Associated Press, April 11, 1985.

Rubenstein, Steve. "Humphrey Caught the Imagination of Thousands." *San Francisco Gate,* May 17, 2007.

Schanberg, Sydney H. "New York: The Land of Hustle and Con." *New York Times,* April 13, 1985.

Vettel, Phil. "Telling the Living Truth About the Unicorn." *Chicago Tribune,* October 18, 1985.

Zell, Timothy G. Surgical procedure. US Patent 4, 429,685, filed July 14, 1982 and issued February 7, 1984.

KOKO

Associated Press. "Efforts to Teach Chimps Draws Mixture of Results." *Tuscaloosa News,* November 2, 1980.

Morin, Roc. "A Conversation with Koko the Gorilla." *Atlantic Monthly,* July/August 2015.

Nature Presents: A Conversation with Koko. DVD. 1999; Chicago: Questar Video, 2004.

Patterson, Francine, and Eugene Linden. *The Education of Koko.* New York: Holt, Rinehart and Winston, 1981.

Patterson, Francine, and Ronald H. Cohn. "Language Acquisition by a Lowland Gorilla." *Word* 41, no. 2 (1990).

"Transcript of the Chat with Koko, 4/27/98." *University of New*

Hampshire. http://pubpages.unh.edu/~jel/kokotranscript
.html.

Wise, Steven M. *Drawing the Line: Science and the Case for Animal Rights.* Cambridge, MA: Perseus Books, 2002.

OSAMA

Associated Press. "Jaguar Had Violent Brother." *Denver Post,* February 26, 2007.

Blomfield, Adrian. "Osama, Terror of Lake Victoria, is Caught at Last." *London Telegraph,* March 13, 2005. Accessed June 16, 2016. http://www.telegraph.co.uk/news/worldnews/africa andindianocean/uganda/1485547/Osama-terror-of-Lake-Victoria-is-caught-at-last.html.

Caputo, Philip. *Ghosts of Tsavo: Stalking the Mystery Lions of East Africa.* Washington, DC: National Geographic Adventure Press, 2002.

Conroy, Scott. "Elephant Named After Bin Laden Shot Dead." *CBS News Online,* December 17, 2006. http://www.cbsnews .com/news/elephant-named-after-bin-laden-shot-dead/.

Graham, Alistair, and Peter Beard. *Eyelids of Morning: The Mingled Destinies of Crocodiles and Men.* New York: A&W Visual Library, 1973.

Kruuk, Hans. *Hunter and Hunted: Relationships Between Carnivores and People.* Cambridge: Cambridge University Press, 2002.

Mitchell, Kirk. "Zoo Mourns Mauled Keeper." *Denver Post,* February 24, 2007.

"Osama's Rampage Ends in Capture." *Washington Times*, March 12, 2005.

Orizio, Riccardo. "Idi Amin's Exile Dream." *New York Times*, August 21, 2003.

Patterson, John Henry. *The Man-Eaters of Tsavo*. New York: Macmillan, 1908. Ebook edition.

Quammen, David. *Monster of God*. New York: Norton, 2003.

Tucker, Abigal. "The Most Ferocious Man-Eating Lions." *Smithsonian Online*, December 16, 2009. http://www.smithsonian mag.com/science-nature/the-most-ferocious-man-eating -lions-2577288/.

Winch, Gordon. *Conquering Comprehension Book 6*. Glebe, Australia: New Frontier Publishing, 2011. Ebook edition.

Wylie, Dan. *Crocodile*. London: Reaktion Books, 2013.

CELIA

Archer, Michael. 2013. "Second Chance for Tasmanian Tigers and Fantastic Frogs." Paper Presented at *TedxDe-extinction*, Washington, D.C., March 15, 2013. *Revive and Restore*. http://reviverestore.org/events/tedxdeextinction/.

Bakalar, Nicholas. "Last Mammoths Spent Final Years on Solitary Island." *New York Times*, May 4, 2015.

Brand, Stewart. "Rethinking Extinction." *Aeon*, April 21, 2015. https://aeon.co/essays/we-are-not-edging-up-to-a-mass -extinction.

Burrow, Mark. *Nature's Ghosts: Confronting Extinction from the Age of Jefferson to the Age of Ecology.* Chicago: University of Chicago Press, 2009.

Church, George. 2013. "Hybridizing Earth with Extinct Species." Paper Presented at *TedxDe-extinction,* Washington, D.C., March 15, 2013. *Revivie and Restore.* http://reviverestore.org/events/tedxdeextinction/.

Church, George. *Regenesis: How Synthetic Biology Will Reinvent Nature and Ourselves.* New York: Basic Books, 2014.

Ehrenfeld, David. 2013. "Extinction Reversal? Don't Count On It." Paper Presented at *TedxDe-extinction,* Washington, D.C., March 15, 2013. *Revivie and Restore.* http://reviverestore.org/events/tedxdeextinction/.

Ellis, Richard. *No Turning Back: The Life and Death of Animal Species.* New York: Harper Perennial, 2004.

Fernández-Árias, Alberto. 2013. "The First De-extinction." Paper Presented at *TedxDe-extinction,* Washington, D.C., March 15, 2013. *Revivie and Restore.* http://reviverestore.org/events/tedxdeextinction/.

Folch, J., Cocero, M. J., Chesné, P., Alabart, J. L., Domínguez, V., Cognié, Y., Roche, A., et al. "First Birth of an Animal from an Extinct Subspecies (*Capra pyrenaica pyrenaica*) by Cloning." *Theriogenology* 71: 2009, 1026-1034.

Galasso, Samantha. "When the Last Great Auks Died, It Was by the Crush of a Fisherman's Boot." *Smithsonian,* July 7, 2014.

http://www.smithsonianmag.com/smithsonian-institution
/with-crush-fisherman-boot-the-last-great-auks-died
=180951982/.

Kolbert, Elizabeth. *The Sixth Extinction: An Unnatural History.* New
York: Henry Holt, 2014.

Lewis, Danny. "The Last Wooly Mammoths Died Isolated and
Alone." *Smithsonian.* May 8, 2015. http://www.smithsonian
mag.com/smart-news/last-wooly-mammoths-died-isolated
-and-alone.

Maas, Peter. "Aurochs: *Bos primigenius.*" *The Sixth Extinction.* August
12, 2014. http://www.petermaas.nl/extinct/speciesinfo
/aurochs.htm.

Novak, Ben. 2013. "How to Bring Passenger Pigeons All the Way
Back." Paper Presented at *TedxDe-extinction,* Washington,
March 15, 2013. *Revive and Restore.* http://reviverestore.org
/events/tedxdeextinction/.

O'Connor: M. R. *Resurrection Science: Conservation, De-extinction and
the Precarious Future of Wild Things.* New York: St. Martin's, 2014.

Shapiro, Beth. 2013. "Ancient DNA: What it is and What it Could
Be." Paper Presented at *TedxDe-extinction,* Washington, March
15, 2013. *Revive and Restore.* http://reviverestore.org/events
/tedxdeextinction/.

---. *How to Clone a Mammoth: the Science of de-Extinction.* Princeton,
NJ: Princeton University Press, 2015.

Rich, Nathaniel. "The Mammoth Cometh." *New York Times,*
February 27, 2014.

Rincon, Paul. "Fresh Effort to Clone Animal." *BBC News,*
November 22, 2013.

Webster, Robert M. and Bruce Erickson. "The Last Word?" *Nature,*
April 4, 1996.

"World's Last Polynesian Tree Snail Dies." *Los Angeles Times,*
February 1, 1996.

Zimmer, Carl. "Bringing Them Back to Life." *National Geographic,*
April 2013.

Zimov, Sergey. "Segey Zimov's Manifesto." *Revive and Restore,*
November 25, 2014. http://reviverestore.org/projects
/woolly-mammoth/sergey-zimovs-manifesto/.

Zitner, Aaron. "Cloned Goat Would Revive Extinct Line." *Los
Angeles Times,* December 24, 2000.

CECIL
"Full Transcript: Walter Palmer Speaks about Cecil the Lion
Controversy." *Minneapolis Star Tribune*, Sept. 7, 2015.

Acknowledgments

Once again, I owe so very much to Sarah Gorham and her team and I am beyond proud to run with the Sarabande pack.

I am extremely grateful to the Whiting Foundation, to the Oregon Literary Fellowships, and to the Oregon State University Center for the Humanities for their generous support of my writing. Thank you for making this project possible.

Much appreciation to the journals and anthologies in which earlier versions of some essays appeared: *Passages North* ("Harriet"), *Cat Is Art Spelled Wrong* ("Jeoffry"), *Oxford American* ("Arabella") and *Virginia Quarterly Review* ("Vogel Staar").

Thank you to Oregon State University's School of Writing, Literature, and Film, especially my fellow Creative Writing faculty. Extra howls of thanks to my spirit animal, the ferocious Professor Marjorie Sandor.

I made it through this project by asking a lot of stupid questions, which were patiently entertained by my friends and colleagues: Tara Williams, Rebecca Olson, Evan Gottlieb, Clement Hawes, Joy Futrell, John D'Agata, Tracy Daugherty, Monica McFawn, Justin St. Germain, and many others I hope to remember later and thank in person. Special thanks to Randa Jarrar for her work translating the videos used in the Bab Amr Bird section of "War Pigs" and to Mark Burford for helping me with the music theory passages in "Vogel Staar."

Many thanks to my students in the MFA programs at OSU and Murray State University, who keep me thinking.

Thanks to Jon Lewis and Irene Taylor Brodsky for saving my laptop and all my notebooks when I accidentally left them seventy miles from home on a freezing porch by the railroad tracks. Whoops.

Thanks to my family: the Passarellos, the Turkels, and Karen Horton; and thanks to Caroline Casey, Patrick Jordan, Riley Hanick, Matthew Gavin Frank, David Conrad, and Alexi Morrissey, who feel more like family every year.

Hooray for the three greatest creatures in history: Charlene, Columbo, and Sharky.

And I am so grateful every damn day for David Turkel, who doesn't (seem to) mind talking to me about animals for the majority of his waking hours, and who guards my heart and my brain like some kind of crazed wolverine.

Wendy Madar

Elena Passarello is the recipient of a 2015 Whiting Award. Her first collection with Sarabande Books, *Let Me Clear My Throat*, won the gold medal for nonfiction at the 2013 Independent Publisher Awards and was a finalist for the 2014 Oregon Book Award. Her essays on performance, pop culture, and the natural world have been published in *Oxford American*, *Slate*, *Creative Nonfiction*, and *The Iowa Review*, among other publications, as well as in the 2015 anthologies *Cat is Art Spelled Wrong* and *After Montaigne: Contemporary Essayists Cover the Essays*. Passarello lives in Corvallis, Oregon and teaches at Oregon State University.

SARABANDE BOOKS is a nonprofit literary press located in Louisville, KY, and Brooklyn, NY. Founded in 1994 to champion poetry, short fiction, and essay, we are committed to creating lasting editions that honor exceptional writing. For more information, please visit sarabandebooks.org.